POET AND POLITICIAN OF PUERTO RICO

Luis Muñoz Marín around the time he wrote "The Pamphlet."

▲▲

POET AND POLITICIAN OF PUERTO RICO
Don Luis Muñoz Marín

▲▲

by Carmen T. Bernier-Grand

To the Tillamook County students/readers:

Let's walk together
toward the great dawn.

Cariños,

[signature]

ORCHARD BOOKS

New York

ACKNOWLEDGMENTS

The research for this biography was made possible by the Society of Children's Book Writers and Illustrators' Anna Cross Giblin 1992 nonfiction grant. I used the grant to travel to Puerto Rico, and I thank them.

Thanks also to my editor, Harold Underdown, who embraced this biography from its beginnings, and to the helpful members of my critique groups. For special help with the research of this book, I am indebted to biographers Carmelo Rosario Natal and Elfren Bernier; the director of Centro de Investigaciones Históricas, María Dolores Luque; the director of the University of Puerto Rico archives, Juan J. González Correa; Georgetown University's archivist, Jon Reynolds; Don Luis Muñoz Marín's former assistant, Enrique Rodríquez Santiago; and Professor Gloria Arjona, who sent me photographs of Doña Muna Lee and answered many of my questions. Profesora Luque also read a draft of the book and suggested corrections. My special gratitude goes to Luis Muñoz Lee, who granted me an interview and made me feel like part of the Muñoz family. And *mil gracias* to the Luis Muñoz Marín Foundation's executive director, Carlos Ruiz Nazario, and its archivists, Julio Quirós Alcalá and Giannina Delgado, for the unlimited use of their time, for archival materials, and for allowing me to walk where Luis Muñoz Marín walked—his home, his office, his garden.

Photographs appear courtesy of the Luis Muñoz Marín Foundation, with the exception of those on the following pages, credits for which are individually noted. Pages 17, 18: Georgetown University archives. Page 34: Gloria Arjona. Page 50: Jack Delano. Page 55: UPI/Bettmann. Page 74: Charles Rotkin. Page 82: Enrique Rodríguez. Page 90: Jack Delano.

All poetry excerpts appear courtesy of Editorial Edil.

Orchard Books, 95 Madison Avenue, New York, NY 10016

Manufactured in the United States of America
Book design by Constance Ftera. The text of this book is set in 12 point Sabon.
The illustrations are black-and-white photographs.

10 9 8 7 6 5 4 3 2 1

Library of Congress Cataloging-in-Publication Data
Bernier-Grand, Carmen T.   Poet and politician of Puerto Rico : Don Luis Muñoz Marín / by Carmen T. Bernier-Grand.   p.   cm. Includes bibliographical references and index. ISBN 0-531-06887-0. — ISBN 0-531-08737-9 (lib. bdg.) 1. Muñoz Marín, Luis, 1898–   —Juvenile literature. 2. Puerto Rico—History—1952–   —Juvenile literature. 3. Statesmen—Puerto Rico—Biography —Juvenile literature. 4. Governors—Puerto Rico—Biography—Juvenile literature. [1. Muñoz Marín, Luis, 1898–   . 2. Puerto Rico—Biography.] I. Title. F1976.3.M86B48 1995 972.9505′3′092—dc20   [B]   94–21985

To my uncle, Elfren Bernier, whose teachings about Muñoz inspired me; to my very Republican parents, José Segundo Bernier Santiago and Julia Rodríguez de Bernier; and to my husband, Jeremy Grand, who pays my taxes

In memory of Sergeant Julio Quirós Rosa, Luis Muñoz Marín's guard, who shared his memories of Muñoz with me

Contents

POET AND POLITICIAN OF PUERTO RICO

At the Birth of a New Century

ㅿㅿ

1898–1900

I was born at the birth of a new century;
at the edge of several decisive events;
at the same moment of the biggest turn
in the history of Puerto Rico. . . .

On February 10, 1898, Governor General Manuel Macías Casado appointed a cabinet in Puerto Rico. The Caribbean island was still a colony of Spain, but for the first time in four hundred years, it had its own government, its autonomy.

Eight days later, José Luis Alberto Muñoz Marín was born in San Juan, the capital of Puerto Rico. His father, Luis Muñoz Rivera, had worked hard for Puerto Rican self-government. He was a poet and journalist as well as a politician. He owned *La Democracia* in Ponce and later *El Diario* in San Juan, newspapers in which he spoke out for Puerto Rico to have self-government now and independence in the near future. He had traveled to Spain to ask for autonomy. Finally Spain had agreed, in part due to the growing conflict with the United States.

Luis Muñoz Rivera was a proud man. He had a son, his small mountainous island had a government run by Puerto Ricans, and he became the most celebrated person in Puerto Rico, the prime minister.

His joy didn't last. Just after five o'clock on the morning of May 12, Puerto Rico had its first taste of the Spanish-American War. A fleet of seven U.S. warships opened fire on San Juan.

José Luis's baptismal notice reads, José Luis Alberto. Born on February 18, 1898. Baptized at the Holy Cathedral Church of San Juan, Puerto Rico, on April 17, 1898. Parents Don Luis Muñoz Rivera and Doña Amalia Marín Castilla. Godparents Don Ramón Marín [uncle] and Doña Loarina Marín Castilla [aunt].

JOSÉ LUIS ALBERTO
Nació
EL 18 DE FEBRERO DE 1898

Bautizado
en la Santa Iglesia Catedral
de
San Juan de Puerto-Rico
el 17 de Abril de 1898

PADRES
D. Luis Muñoz Rivera
Dª Amalia Marín Castilla

PADRINOS
D. Ramón Marín
Dª Loarina Marín Castilla

Sucesión de J. J. Acosta

"THE FIRST FLASH OF FIRE AND SMOKE"

José Luis was three months old when the United States opened fire on El Morro in San Juan, Puerto Rico.

José Luis's mother, Doña Amalia Marín de Muñoz, snatched José Luis from his crib and took him inland to the town of Río Piedras. José Luis's father stayed in San Juan, moving other families away from the bay. None of that was necessary. One shell landed deep in a wall of El Morro, but the fort held out. After three hours, the American ships left the north coast of Puerto Rico, and José Luis returned to sleep in his own crib.

But the United States would not give up Puerto Rico. The Caribbean was essential for rapid communication between the Atlantic and Pacific oceans, and the island's strategic location was ideal for U.S. naval stations.

On July 25, U.S. troops landed at the southern coast town of Guánica. There was no resistance.

Many Puerto Ricans received the troops with parades and music, opened their homes to them, and gave them cigars and bananas. "Long live the Americans!" the islanders shouted. Their hopes were high. They thought they could now move more quickly toward their goal of independence, or to better conditions as part of the United States. But the island had enjoyed more freedom under the Spanish than it was about to enjoy under U.S. rule.

When José Luis was born, Puerto Rico was mostly rural. There were merchants, sugar and coffee planters, lawyers, and doctors who made up the ruling class of which his father was part. Agriculture was by far the leading industry. The land was divided into large plantations and small farms cultivated by Puerto Ricans. They exported coffee, tobacco, and sugar. The main towns had a railroad, telegraph, and several newspapers. There was much illiteracy and poverty, but these problems were also common in many parts of the United States.

Nevertheless, the Americans measured Puerto Rico by their own standards. They saw Puerto Ricans as people who desperately needed to be taught the American culture, American government, and the English language so they could be better off in life.

On December 10, 1898, Spain signed the Treaty of Paris, ceding Puerto Rico to the United States. Shortly after, Luis Muñoz Rivera wrote in *La Democracia* that he hoped the United States would respect the island's hard-won autonomy. The new governor of Puerto Rico, General Guy V. Henry, did not like the comments coming from *La Democracia* and stopped it from being printed. Although censorship and a military government were against democracy, this was the way Puerto Rico was ruled for two years.

In 1900, Congress passed the Foraker Act. No Puerto Ricans had had a say in what went into it. Under this law, Puerto Rico was made a colony of the United States.

All that was left from Luis Muñoz Rivera's ten years of negotiations with Spain was the memory of four months of autonomy. Yet it was this memory that sparked José Luis's father to work tirelessly for a return to autonomy. Deep inside, Muñoz Rivera preferred full independence. But he was a practical man and wanted to take one step at a time.

His friend José Celso Barbosa had now left the autonomy movement. Barbosa, who had studied medicine at the University of Michigan, had wonderful memories of the wealth, progress, and political freedom he had found in the United States. Under the Spanish rule, he had worked—sometimes with Luis Muñoz Rivera—to stress equality through autonomy. Barbosa now sought equality through statehood.

Another opponent of autonomy was the leader of the Puerto Rican labor movement, Santiago Iglesias. Both Muñoz Rivera and Iglesias wanted to help the urban workers and the mountain peasants called *jíbaros*. But José Luis's father and Iglesias never understood each other, especially not now when Iglesias was seeking guidance from the American Socialist Party and, like Barbosa, working for statehood.

The status issue—whether Puerto Rico should become a state, independent, or autonomous—was a burning question when José Luis was a baby, and has been debated ever since. It is not only a question of identity—whether the islanders are Americans, Puerto Ricans, or both—but also a question of economics and well-being.

In 1900 and for many years afterward, most Puerto Ricans believed that if they resolved the status issue, they could then solve their social and economic problems.

The political status of the island was discussed night after night in the Muñoz home. These conversations were the bedtime stories that put José Luis to sleep—until he was three.

An Upside-down Sky

⋀⋀

1900–1905

Our Father who art in heaven . . .
Make harmony among men and nature. . . .

José Luis grew up listening to his father and his father's friends talking about politics. When he was three, a parade of pro-statehood Republicans—supporters of José Celso Barbosa—passed by the house.

José Luis shouted, "Death to Barbosa!"

Muñoz Rivera asked José Luis to shout, "Long live Barbosa." Politics aside, José Celso Barbosa was his friend. But even if he wasn't, Muñoz Rivera didn't want his son to wish death to anybody.

"Long live Barbosa!" José Luis shouted.

This way of relating to people and wishing them a good life stayed in José Luis's mind.

Shortly after the Barbosa incident, the Republicans broke into *El Diario*. They didn't like the articles Luis Muñoz Rivera wrote

Could this have been José Luis's swimsuit? Perhaps, but photographers often supplied the settings and costumes for their customers. The painted beach background is missing the Puerto Rican palm trees.

supporting autonomy. So they scattered the type all over the street and left the printing press beyond repair. The incident made the family move to Caguas, a mountain town. And Muñoz Rivera moved with him his other newspaper, *La Democracia*.

José Luis loved the familiar smell of ink at *La Democracia* and the sound of the rotary press. He also enjoyed riding the merry-go-round at the Caguas plaza, and pretending to ride the wheelless coach that belonged to the saddlemaker.

But as José Luis's father continued to write his articles, the family received more and more threats from the Republicans. The day came when José Luis's mother dressed him up in boots, gloves, and a beret, and they set out to move to New York. On the train ride from Caguas to San Juan to board the ship *Philadelphia*, the wind blew José Luis's white cap off his head.

"The hat landed in a creek," José Luis said later. "It looked like the moon floating on an upside-down sky."

Soon José Luis was playing in the New York streets and parks with American children. He learned English quickly and spoke it without an accent. Puerto Rico, however, was in the apartments where he lived and spoke Spanish. He grew up bilingual, and his sense of belonging in New York and Puerto Rico helped him understand both—his American and his Puerto Rican friends. His father also taught him his belief that "there is not such a thing as 'we' and 'them.' You must learn to be an American among Americans, a Puerto Rican among Puerto Ricans, a human being among human beings."

So José Luis listened carefully to what everyone had to say. Most of the time, he looked straight at the person speaking. But sometimes, while he listened to a conversation, his eyes moved fast, as if they were butterflies flying over everything. Whenever he was given the opportunity, he asked questions such as, "What is the name of that flower?" "How cold can it get here?" "Where can I buy that book?" He was an avid reader. His favorite books were *The Three Musketeers* and *Robinson Crusoe*.

Sometimes José Luis went with his father to the Café Martín, where people who came from Puerto Rico gave them news about the island. As José Luis put it, "My father was a protagonist of something that was not in New York."

And so Luis Muñoz Rivera was constantly traveling from New York to Puerto Rico, from Puerto Rico to New York. When he was in New York, his mind and his time were dedicated to freeing the island from its problems. Yet he couldn't stay in colonial Puerto Rico, a feeling he had tried to explain in this poem written when Puerto Rico was a Spanish possession:

> *I was not born to emit the note*
> *of the nightingale in the city enslaved;*
> *I am going to rough and unknown regions;*
> *At the end, I will arrive with broken wings;*
> *But at the end, I know, I will arrive.*

Soon Puerto Rico's pro-statehood Republicans became as unhappy with the enslaving, colonial situation of the island as Muñoz Rivera was. José Luis's father thought then that if Puerto Ricans could form a single party, they would be strong enough to press the United States for a better deal. On one of his trips to Puerto Rico, he founded the Unionist Party to press for autonomy. Some Republicans joined him. In November 1904, the party won the election and, therefore, most of the House of Delegates seats. Luis Muñoz Rivera became a delegate. So José Luis and his mother began to plan their return trip to Puerto Rico.

If I Were a Tree

ᴧᴧᴧ

1905–1910

*. . . The green foliage that shoots out
from your trunk is not enough
to express your whole soul. . . .*

On August 3, 1905, José Luis and his mother arrived in Puerto Rico. His father met them at the docks with a carriage. José Luis later described his feelings on that day by saying, "San Juan, where the horseshoes broke the silence of the cobblestones on the streets, was home!"

Soon after their return, José Luis had an experience that he never forgot. He was playing with some new friends at the corner of Tetuán Street when a vendor, selling snow cones, parked his cart and called, "*¡Piraguas!*"

José Luis ordered *piraguas* for himself and his friends. He paid for them and was about to put the leftover penny in his pocket when a beggar called, "A penny for the poor!"

José Luis gave him the penny and sat on the curb to eat the *piragua.* When he was done, the vendor called again, "*¡Piraguas!*"

José Luis bought seconds, and the beggar called again, "A penny for the poor!" José Luis gave him another penny. This continued until he ran out of money.

Later, when José Luis told of the incident, he shrugged and said, "If some people could eat *piraguas*, it seemed natural to me that others could eat bread."

Although Muñoz Rivera was a famous politician in the island, he taught José Luis that he wasn't superior to anybody. "I don't remember belonging to any class," José Luis said. "I was a person growing up among people—Americans, Puerto Ricans, shoe shiners, manufacturers, merchants, *jíbaros*."

The *jíbaros* were the mountain peasants. Muñoz Rivera's hometown was Barranquitas, which is in the mountains, and José Luis saw the poor *jíbaros* often. American companies were buying most of the small farms to develop them into large sugar plantations, leaving the *jíbaros* almost no land to cultivate. The *jíbaros* lived in straw shacks, ate dried codfish, and slept in hammocks. Most of them couldn't read or write.

Around this time, José Luis began first grade at William Penn Public School in Santurce. All subjects were taught in English in the public schools of Puerto Rico, though most Puerto Ricans couldn't speak it. José Luis was too advanced for first grade. He was moved to the second grade, where the Puerto Rican teacher hadn't mastered English.

"Seven plus seven is *fortin*," the teacher said.

And the students tried to repeat, "Seven plus seven is *foltin*."

When José Luis said "fourteen," his classmates laughed, perhaps thinking he was wrong.

"It is the way José Luis says it," the teacher said. But she didn't repeat the word.

José Luis passed second grade, but not third. The teacher told his

José Luis around the time of first grade. For boys in the 1900s, suits with knee-length trousers were popular. Military symbols—embroidered eagles, stripes, anchors, and stars—were common.

parents that he had a short attention span and a lack of interest. José Luis did daydream a lot. For instance, he daydreamed he was a writer covering a historical moment for *La Democracia*. He made up stories and wrote headlines: JAPAN TAKES OVER SAN JUAN. PRESIDENT THEODORE ROOSEVELT IN BAYAMÓN TO DEFEND THE ISLAND OF PUERTO RICO. Sometimes he sent the stories to *La Democracia*.

That summer his parents took him to Barranquitas and hired a private teacher for him. As soon as his father paid the full amount for the classes in advance, the teacher disappeared. José Luis had a fun summer, after all, and he learned a great deal that wasn't taught in schools.

The mayor of Barranquitas loaned José Luis his horse, and his parents agreed to let him enjoy the countryside. Most days, José Luis rode on mountain roads as curvy as hairpins. He stopped here and there to hear the *jíbaros* tell stories.

"I found out the secrets of the river, mysterious ghosts and fairies," José Luis said in his autobiography, "and about the mail carrier who fell down a waterfall called Salto Padilla."

José Luis felt at home among the *jíbaros* and in the natural world. He used to say he spoke to the trees, and the trees understood him. Once he wrote:

> *I understand and I smile*
> *I sing what you would sing*
> *If you were a poet.*
> *I know it.*
> *Because if I were a tree*
> *My branches would send out shoots like yours.*

In 1908, José Luis went to a small private school on Sol Street in San Juan. His teacher was Pedro Moczó, a warm, loving man who taught mostly in Spanish and understood José Luis well. At least once Moczó sent a note to José Luis's father:

> Your son is undisciplined but very bright. He doesn't care about grades; he just wants knowledge.

José Luis's father answered:

> My observations of José Luis and his school improvements agree with the report you sent me. I believe he is intelligent but also that his negligence is great and difficult to correct.
>
> In the last year, he has improved a great deal. And if from the very beginning he'd been under your direction, I'm sure he'd have knowledge superior for his age. Now we can only try to gain the lost time.

José Luis had been bored in the other schools because he had to wait for his peers to catch up. Pedro Moczó didn't make him wait. In two years, José Luis covered all the material from third to eighth grade. And he got good grades.

Joe Rivera

1910–1916

Tell me,
Umbrella-mongers,
When has an umbrella ever
Kept the rain and the mist from entering a heart
And shaking it with dreams?

At the beginning of 1910, José Luis's father was elected Puerto Rico's resident commissioner in the United States. His job required him to live in Washington, D.C. José Luis's mother refused to move to the nation's capital. She preferred to go to New York to be near her sister. At first José Luis moved back to New York with his mother. Soon, though, his father insisted that José Luis come to study at Georgetown Preparatory School, where politicians' sons studied.

At Georgetown his schoolmates and teachers knew José Luis as "Joe Rivera." The new name began when on September 13, 1911, the registration clerk wrote in the entrance book:

> Rivera, Joseph Louis Muñoz. San Juan, Porto Rico. Son of Hon. Louis Muñoz Rivera. The Benediek, I St., Wash., D.C. (House Bldg., Room 488)

1911 – 12.

Sept. 13. Wagner, Walter Esmond,   B.
           Son of Mrs. Mary E. Wagner.
           # 60 West, 126th Street, New York City, N.Y.

Sept. 13. Shaw, Christopher J., Stapleton.   B.
           Son of Christopher J. Shaw.
           294 Garfield Place, Brooklyn, N.Y.

Sept. 13. Schorn, Franklin Martin,   B.
           209. S. Carroll, Madison, Wis.
           Son of Frank H. Schorn, Wales, Wis.

Sept. 13. Rivera, Joseph Louis Muñoz.   B.
           San Juan, Porto Rico. Son of Hon.
           Louis Muñoz Rivera. The Benedick, I
           St., Wash. D.C. (House Bldg., Room 488.

Sept. 13. O'Day, Francis Joseph Aloysius   D.
           Son of John Jos. O'Day.
           4503 Wisconsin Avenue, Tennallytown, D.C.

Sept. 13. Huglen, Charles Wolfram Joseph.   D.
           2514. 17th St., N.W. Son of Frank Joseph.
           Huglen, 816 - 14th Street, N.W., (Care Mr. King.)

Georgetown Preparatory School's registration page. José Luis's listing is the third from the bottom. The correct way to register him would have been "Muñoz Marín, José Luis."

The clerk probably thought Rivera was his father's surname and so had to be José Luis's surname. He didn't understand that, in Puerto Rico, people put their mother's surname after their father's surname.

From the beginning, José Luis disliked the rigid discipline at Georgetown Preparatory School. Once he and his friends marched, protesting the school discipline. As a result, they were locked in a classroom until they could write an essay about their "bad" behavior in classical Greek.

In the summer of 1914, World War I began in Europe. José Luis couldn't sign up for the army. He was only sixteen and wasn't a U.S. citizen. So he spent his summer vacation in the dance halls on

Georgetown Preparatory School's class picture. José Luis is the sixth student from the right in the first row. He was fourteen.

Broadway, near his mother's home, and enjoying himself at Coney Island.

That September, he was supposed to return to Georgetown to repeat the tenth grade, which he hadn't passed. The 1914 elections, however, kept his father in Puerto Rico until after the beginning of classes, and his mother couldn't persuade him to go to school. When his father returned, it was too late to register. Nevertheless, José Luis moved to Washington, D.C., with his father, where he began what he called the "best University." He typed letters for his father, read books in English and Spanish, and translated a biography of Goya from French into English. He also learned about the history and politics of Puerto Rico and the United States.

In 1915, his father insisted that he study law, and registered him for night classes at Georgetown Law School. It was a waste of time and money. José Luis didn't study. He had dreams like those his father had had. Muñoz Rivera's father had wanted him to be a businessman. But very early in life, Muñoz Rivera had drifted away from those plans to become a poet. Now José Luis was doing the same. He was moving away from studying law to write poems.

One of his Georgetown classmates once said that José Luis "always behaved like a poet. At lunch, he would stop eating and stare into space. Sometimes he would get so absentminded that he would scratch his head with his fork." But José Luis described his first poem as "one that was so bad that all I can remember is that it was bad."

José Luis often went to parties until 2:00 A.M. His father usually waited for him. Sitting on a yellow leather chair, he advised José Luis not to party so much. Then father and son talked long into the night.

"One night, Muñoz Rivera explained international socialism to me," José Luis said later.

His father talked about what was going on in France, Britain, Germany, and Russia. But Muñoz Rivera was not a socialist. He wanted autonomy for Puerto Rico and was having difficulties getting it.

Representative William Jones from Virginia had introduced a bill to grant Puerto Ricans American citizenship. Jones also proposed to make Puerto Ricans eligible for the U.S. military draft and to establish a Senate elected by Puerto Ricans. This was a step forward, but there was a problem. Most *jíbaros* couldn't read or write. Therefore, the Jones Bill said, they couldn't vote.

Muñoz Rivera gave speeches asking for amendments to the bill to allow the *jíbaros* to vote. But it was the citizenship issue that worried him the most. He said that the citizenship was going to be in name only because it denied Puerto Ricans their right to elect members of Congress.

José Luis said his country would always be Puerto Rico. But if the Jones Bill should pass, his citizenship would be "that of Puerto Rico and that of the United States."

Yet he helped his father practice his speeches and spent many hours correcting his pronunciation. "I wanted my father to win his second battle," José Luis said years later. "I wanted him to win the second autonomy for Puerto Rico."

Muñoz Rivera had gotten the first autonomy from Spain and seen it lost when the Americans invaded Puerto Rico. The Jones Bill was the closest he could get to it a second time.

Death of a Giant

1916

. . . The bells toll, and toll,
and continue tolling at great length
and each bell rips apart
the heart of each Puerto Rican.

By September 1916, José Luis knew the Jones Bill would pass with most of his father's amendments. The United States agreed to give citizenship to Puerto Ricans, but didn't allow them the right to elect representatives to Congress. Nevertheless, the island could have a Senate. And Puerto Ricans could vote for it, even if they couldn't read or write.

José Luis wanted to go to Puerto Rico with his father and celebrate, but his father didn't let him go. José Luis had to stay in Washington and go to Georgetown Law School.

As José Luis expected, a large crowd welcomed his father to Puerto Rico. They cheered him and called him their hero. It was a moment of victory, but the joy didn't last. Two days later, a family friend, Eduardo Georgetti, called. José Luis and his mother had to come to Puerto Rico right away. Muñoz Rivera's gallbladder had

Luis Muñoz Rivera wears a fashionable straw hat called a boater, on his return to Puerto Rico from Washington, D.C. Antonio Barceló is to his right.

burst, and the infection had spread to his whole body. Georgetti had offered to pay for the most expensive treatments, but nothing could be done. José Luis's father was dying.

As soon as José Luis and his mother got there, Muñoz Rivera gave Georgetti instructions on how to take care of his son and wife. José Luis had to finish his law degree. They could pay the tuition if they sold some land he owned and used the $5,000 from his life insurance. That and whatever was in his checkbook was his whole fortune. He left it to Georgetti's generosity to supply whatever else was needed.

On November 15, 1916, at the age of fifty-seven, Don Luis Muñoz Rivera died. His death produced in José Luis "a strong commotion, a desperate anguish." Outside their home, the church bells tolled for the dead. People sang the Puerto Rican anthem, "*La Borinqueña*," then cried, "Muñoz hasn't died. He'll always live in our hearts. Long live Muñoz!"

Five days later, the funeral procession moved slowly from Santurce to San Juan, from San Juan to Ponce, and from Ponce to Barranquitas, where José Luis's father wanted to be buried. It was

Luis Muñoz Rivera's funeral procession leaves San Juan.

After his father's death, José Luis wrote a piece that appeared with this photo in the magazine Juan Bobo.

then José Luis understood how much his father had meant to hundreds of thousands of Puerto Ricans. *Jíbaros* poured from every town, from every road, from every mountain to mourn for him. Many of them walked, and José Luis walked with them.

"How much he loved Puerto Rico!" José Luis said that day. "And how much Puerto Rico loved him!"

A few days later, José Luis wrote this piece, which was published in the magazine *Juan Bobo* with a picture of him standing by his father's tomb:

> *I would like to be a giant*
> *to embrace the mountains that he contemplated*
> *in his boyhood,*
> *the mountains for which he struggled from his youth onward*
> *the mountains that sheltered his countrymen, the* jíbaros,
> *and that today entomb his body.*
> *I would like to be a giant*
> *to hold close to my chest all these Puerto Ricans*
> *who keep forever in their noble hearts*
> *the sacred memory of my father.*
> *And I would like to be a giant.*
> *to complete the work of Luis Muñoz Rivera,*
> *the giant of Borinquén.*

But José Luis was not a giant yet. Many years would pass before he could continue his father's work.

The Bohemian Poet

<<<<<<<<<<<<<<<<<<<<<<<<<<<<<<<<<<<<<<<<<<<<<<

1916–1918

This vulgar world of five senses bores me
like a dog that slowly licks the hand
his owner extends indifferently. . . .

A month after his father's death, José Luis and his mother sailed to New York. There José Luis sold his law books and refused to return to Georgetown. His mood was such that his mother wrote a letter to his uncle who lived in Puerto Rico:

> A few lines to let you know about my son. He has a good nature. The death of his father has made such an impression on his spirit that his behavior has changed completely. We were concerned because he used to be a partygoer and, today, he's too quiet for his age.

José Luis felt bored and lost without his father. He said in his autobiography that he wanted to know his father's wishes for him

José Luis and his mother at Eduardo Georgetti's house before leaving for New York. Puerto Rican widows wore mourning clothes the rest of their lives. Men wore black ribbons around their arms, but only for a few months.

(other than his becoming a lawyer). Not knowing the answer, José Luis took the path he had wanted to take, that of a writer.

Within a month, he had written most of a book he entitled *Borrones*, "Ink Blots." At the time, people wrote with fountain pens, and sometimes the ink made blots, smudges on the paper. José Luis's book didn't really have ink blots, but he called it that because he felt his work was not as good as that of other writers.

The book included seven serious and humorous stories and a one-act play. "The play," José Luis said, "had been produced many times in the theater of my dreams with great success."

That spring he sailed back to the island to finish and publish his book on *La Democracia*'s press. His mother, who knew that the warmth of Puerto Rico and a few friends would be enough to change her son into a partygoer again, wrote to his uncle:

> You know that girls and boys in the United States are raised with more freedom. That freedom seems excessive to those who are not accustomed to it, and because of that young people who go from New York to Puerto Rico are harshly criticized. Advise José Luis to follow our customs. . . .

Young Puerto Ricans then lived with their parents until they got married. Boys as old as eighteen asked permission to go out, and they came home before midnight. Girls had more restrictions. They never went out without chaperones.

José Luis had grown up mostly in the United States and didn't understand any of that. In Puerto Rico, he joined a group of poets. Tall, suntanned, and handsome, José Luis spent the days with the young men, swimming and watching elegant and playful ladies at Parque Borinquén.

Sometimes he became serious. He buried his feet in the shining white sand and recited works such as those of his favorite North American poet, Edwin Markham:

THE MAN WITH THE HOE

Bowed by the weight of centuries he leans
Upon his hoe and gazes on the ground,
The emptiness of ages in his face,
And on his back the burden of the world.

Markham's poem inspired José Luis to write poems about the *jíbaros*. But it was difficult to separate the *jíbaro* of a poem from the *jíbaro* in Puerto Rican politics. In the evenings, the young poets talked about the burden of the *jíbaro* with machete and hoe. They switched to the injustices caused by the American governor and landowners. And they ended up loudly discussing the political status of Puerto Rico.

As his mother feared, Puerto Ricans criticized José Luis. They called him the "bohemian poet" because he pretended to be a writer—though his *Borrones* were truly "ink blots"; because he dressed in a careless way; and because he didn't behave the way a young Puerto Rican of an illustrious family should behave. They said that José Luis had Americanized himself and had lost touch with Puerto Rican realities.

The idle talk made José Luis so angry that he wrote:

Blessed is Puerto Rico, blessed are the palm trees that shade its emerald fields, blessed are the blue seas that wash its beaches, and the mountains that house the *jíbaro*, blessed is its blue sky like a child's dream, and the sun that warms our veins, our Latin blood, blessed are all of these, yes; but damned, one thousand times damned, is the crushing, ridiculous, dated, narrowed point of view under which we are born, live, and die!

José Luis as a "Bohemian Poet." He dedicated this photo to his mother, whom he called Maló.

Most Puerto Ricans, especially Antonio Barceló, now leader of the Unionist Party, expected him to be like his father and also called him "the son of Muñoz Rivera."

"I have an honorable name," José Luis said in response. "But the name doesn't glorify me. My father earned that glory, and it belongs to him."

Then they said that José Luis hated his father. They couldn't understand that the nights of talk and poetry were allowing him to find himself inside the Puerto Rican issue.

The first step to search for one's identity is to find one's name. After finding that name, it's easier to find one's own answers, one's own style, one's own sense of belonging.

José Luis had found his name. He now called himself Luis Muñoz Marín.

New York

1918–1920

Talkative city of one-thousand dialogues

In 1918, Luis Muñoz Marín moved to Greenwich Village in New York, where he spent most of his time writing. "When I knew I could [write], I knew I was a free man," he recalled many years later. He was also free to be the founder and editor of *Revista de Indias*, a magazine of Latin American prose, poetry, and opinion. The first issue came out in August 1918.

While editing the magazine, Muñoz met Muna Lee. She was a small, elegant woman from Mississippi. She had a bachelor's degree in science, could speak Spanish, and was a poet who had won a writer's award from *Poetry* magazine. She was also restless, like Muñoz Marín.

Muñoz and Muna took long walks in Central Park, where he fell as wildly in love with her as she did with him. She wrote about him:

The thought of you is taller than the sunset
Flaming up above the world's crumbling edges.

The thought of you is wilder than the wild birds
Whose only joy is in their own wild flying.

And around this time, he wrote:

These are singing things:
The stars,
The sea,
Lovers.
These are silent things:
The night,
The sand,
Love.

They met in February 1919. By July, they were married. Muna, however, had writing commitments, so they postponed their honeymoon trip.

Every Sunday, a crowd of North American poets visited the couple. Since this was a Puerto Rican home, no one had to be invited. People just came—ready to stay until dawn. Muna offered them crackers with melted cheese topped with paprika. Whenever they could afford it, she served sherry.

Muñoz listened carefully to his poet friends talking about democracy and wrote about them. "What have these men done to connect so fast and so well to their fellow human beings? That's exactly it! They remember that the rest of the men, women, and children *are* their fellow human beings, and not inferior beings to whom everything big and everlasting is prohibited."

Muñoz had been reading books written by socialist theorists Marx and Lenin, and he felt socialism was the best solution for Puerto

Muna Lee.

Rico. But he felt strongly about democracy as well. The *jíbaros* now had the right to vote. Perhaps this could take Puerto Rico out of its poverty.

Muna and Muñoz went to Washington, D.C., and Philadelphia for their honeymoon. They had hardly any money, so they hitchhiked from New York and sometimes walked. In Philadelphia, they ran out of money, and Muna called *Poetry* magazine. Her editors had not paid her for some of her work. Sitting in a park in the rain, Muna and Muñoz waited for the money. When it came, probably by telegram, they continued their adventure on the way back to New York—back to reality.

"You can trade literature for fame," Muñoz said once. "But you cannot trade it for bread." This was turning out to be true in his own life.

Revista de Indias had failed after three issues, and there was even less money for Muna, who was pregnant, and for Muñoz to live on. His mother, now in Puerto Rico, helped them by sending money whenever she could. That was not often enough. Muna and Muñoz couldn't afford to live in Greenwich Village, so they moved to a Puerto Rican carpenter's house on Staten Island, a ferry ride from Manhattan.

Muna was more practical than her husband. She often visited the New York Public Library to research interesting articles that would sell. She wrote essays on international affairs and reviewed books and art for newspapers. She also took care of most of the household matters.

Muñoz dedicated himself to his writing, forgetting, at times, it was important to fix a dripping faucet and to make enough money. Edwin Markham, who had "the white beard of a prophet and a socio-angelical compassion" and who was the author of "The Man with the Hoe," the poem that Muñoz liked so much, lived close by. They visited each other, talked about socialism, and Muñoz translated "The Man with the Hoe" into Spanish.

But after a while Muñoz began to feel restless on Staten Island. At first he wanted to go to Argentina to work on a magazine with Nemesio Canales, one of his Puerto Rican poet friends.

"The trip was not possible," he said later, "because my first son— who turned out to be my first daughter, Munita—was about to be born."

Muñoz decided to go to Puerto Rico instead. He asked Dr. Julio Henna if Muna could go with him. The Irish–Puerto Rican doctor saw no problem with her taking the trip. In addition, Dr. Henna said, "Take this check to Santiago Iglesias. . . . He's the only one trying to help the hungry *jíbaros*."

Excited by the opportunity to meet the leader of the Puerto Rican Socialist Party, Muñoz agreed to deliver the check. Shortly afterward, he and Muna left for Puerto Rico, where Munita was born.

With the Mob of Hungry People

1920

Listen to us, Universe;
Listen to us, God . . .
One time . . . only one time . . .

Soon after Muñoz arrived in Puerto Rico, he learned of the tragic outcome of the Jones Bill. This was the first election year after the bill had passed. As his father had wanted, the illiterate *jíbaros* could now vote. The *jíbaros* appreciated this right, not because they could vote, but because they could sell their vote. They sold it to their coffee, sugar, or tobacco landowners, who voted in place of the *jíbaros*. A vote was worth two dollars.

Muñoz had kept himself loyal to socialism but also loyal to democracy. He cared deeply for civil rights and deplored the selling of votes. The landowners didn't vote in favor of the *jíbaros'* rights. They used the votes they bought to vote for the party that could make them richer.

The Unionists, who had won every election since 1904, and the Republicans were the same when it came to what José Luis felt was important. They disagreed over the political status of Puerto Rico, but both parties saw the *jíbaros* only as votes the landowners could buy. The politicians let the landowners do whatever they wished as long as they bought enough votes for their party to win.

Only one party was with the *jíbaros*: the Socialist Party.

Muñoz took Dr. Henna's check to Santiago Iglesias.

"I want to be a member of the Socialist Party," Muñoz told the leader.

Santiago Iglesias opened his brown eyes wide. "Young man, do you know what you're saying?"

"Yes, comrade."

Santiago Iglesias put his arm around Muñoz's shoulder. "Listen. Your father was a prominent leader of the Unionist Party. Please, don't get yourself in trouble."

"I might be the son of Muñoz Rivera, but I have a mind of my own!"

"All right. Early tomorrow, I am going to the town of Fajardo to check on the strike in the sugarcane fields. If you want, you may come with me. If after that you still want to join the Socialist Party, you may do so."

The next day, Muñoz traveled with Iglesias in a run-down car to the northeast coast of the island. The smooth green carpet of the sugarcane fields near Fajardo looked deserted. The *jíbaros* weren't cutting the cane with their machetes. Only the gentle March breeze moved the plants. Then a man came out of a sugarcane alley and blew an abalone shell. All of a sudden, hundreds of men and women came out of every alley.

"Here comes the strike!" they shouted. The landowners had increased the price of sugar but had not increased the *jíbaros'* $1.00-a-day wages. The strikers were asking for $2.50 a day.

Muñoz went to stand among the workers and listened as Iglesias

A jíbaro *walks on the road between Lajas and the Bay of La Parguera. This photograph was taken in 1937, when photographers had become more interested in the* jíbaros.

Luis Muñoz Marín (left) and Santiago Iglesias on a Socialist Party propaganda piece.

told them, "In organization there's strength." After the speech, another socialist told Iglesias that they needed help to keep the strike alive. Immediately Muñoz offered to stay and help.

"No!" Santiago Iglesias said in a stern voice. "You came with me and you go back with me."

Out of respect for Santiago Iglesias, Muñoz returned to San Juan. At home, he found his mother waiting for him. Somebody had seen him leaving town with Iglesias. And all day long, friends of the family had paraded into the house to console his mother for this "disaster."

As soon as he walked in, his mother asked him if it was true that he had become a socialist. When he admitted it, she tried to play on his feelings, saying her heart was not strong. Muñoz was determined. He told her and all their family friends that he would "act according to my beliefs, just as my father acted according to his."

Between March and October 1920, Luis Muñoz Marín went with Iglesias to more than forty towns. During this brief period together, Iglesias spoke of the right to enjoy reasonable wages, good working conditions, clean housing, schools, hospitals, and other needs that could provide for health, happiness, and dignity. Luis Muñoz Marín listened carefully and absorbed everything. And he followed Iglesias's teachings.

Muñoz came into the towns on foot, strolled through the streets, and talked with people in the plaza. With his rumpled hair, and his wrinkled shirt hanging over his khaki pants, he looked like a *jíbaro*. And the *jíbaros* said he behaved like one of them.

Luis Muñoz Marín gave speeches, but mostly he used his large ears to listen. As he listened and listened, he decided to drown his poet dreams for the dreams of those with bare feet. He wrote about his decision in his poem "The Pamphlet." Although later he went back to his writing, he never abandoned the welfare of the *jíbaros*.

THE PAMPHLET

I have broken the rainbow against my heart
as one breaks a useless sword against a knee.
I have blown the clouds of pink and blood
farther than the last horizons.
I have drowned my dreams
to feed the dreams that sleep for me in the veins
of men who have sweated and wept and raged
to season my coffee . . .
The dream that sleeps in breasts stifled by
tuberculosis
(A little air, a little sunshine!)
the dream that dreams in stomachs cramped by hunger
(A bit of bread, a bit of white bread!)
the dream of bare feet
(Fewer stones on the road, Lord, fewer broken bottles!)
the dream of the horizontal necks
(A roof, leaves, yaguas: the sun is horrible!)
the dream of calloused hands
(Moss . . . clean cambric . . . things smooth, soft, soothing!)
the dream of trampled hearts
(Love . . . Life . . . Life . . . Life!)
I am the pamphleteer of God,
The agitator of God,
And I go with the mob of stars and hungry men
toward the great dawn . . .

Sand and Ashes Were Less Free

1920–1931

Beloved, do not fear to leave me—
I shall not forget you!

Some Puerto Ricans accused Muñoz of being unpatriotic and a Communist. Even so, he stayed with the Socialist Party. In October 1920, however, Santiago Iglesias himself did an abrupt about-face. Saying that he couldn't put in practice his social justice unless the Unionists were defeated, he tried to strengthen his party by accepting many Republicans.

Muñoz was disappointed, though he never forgot Iglesias and his teachings. He moved back to the United States with his mother, his pregnant wife, Muna, and one-year-old Munita. With the money from a small piece of land his mother sold in Puerto Rico, they made a down payment on a house in New Jersey.

"[The house] was in the countryside about ten miles from New York," Muñoz remembered. "It was there where my daughter Munita and my son Luis [Muñoz Lee] spent their first years."

Munita, Muna, and Luis in church.

Although Muñoz didn't say any more in his autobiography about his son's birth, it had to be an important event. Most Puerto Ricans wanted a boy who could pass on the family name. And the previous year, when Munita was born, Muñoz had expected a boy.

Now he had a son. He also found a job writing book reviews, but it didn't pay enough to support the family. They supplemented his salary with a small pension his mother received, the little income she got from *La Democracia*, and what Muna earned from her writing.

In 1923, after three years away, Muñoz decided to return with his family to Puerto Rico. He was going to compile his father's unpublished works in a book entitled *Political Campaigns*. Muna didn't want to follow her husband into an unstable life again. They had children now, and she couldn't come and go as easily anymore.

But Muna didn't want to stop Muñoz from doing what he wanted. In a book entitled *Sea Change*, she wrote:

> *I have had enough of glamour,*
> *Of dawns, and violent dusks, and stars,*
> *Of crimson banners flaming and floating*
> *Over vague and perilous wars.*

And in another poem she told him:

> *I make no question of your right to go—*
> *Rain and swift lightning, thunder and the sea,*
> *Sand and dust and ashes are less free!*
> *Follow all paths that wings and spread sails know,*
> *Unheralded you came, and even so,*
> *If so you will, you may take leave of me.*
> *Yours is your life, and what you will shall be.*
> *I ask no questions: hasten or be slow!*

Muñoz lived in Puerto Rico without his family for almost two years. As he compiled his father's works, he watched Antonio Barceló and the Unionists with interest. Barceló had always wanted independence. But the United States kept on saying it couldn't give Puerto Rico statehood or independence until the island lowered its illiteracy rate. So Barceló's Unionists proposed a new form of autonomy, one in which Puerto Rico could have close ties with the United States, but also could have its own elected governor and its own constitution. They called this new status a "Free Associate State."

Muñoz didn't think this form of autonomy was a "serious solution." "Independence," he said, "though a crazy idea, should always be in the program of a serious party."

In contrast, those Republicans who had not joined Iglesias saw the autonomy formula as a realistic temporary solution. They joined the Unionists and founded the Unionist-Republican Alliance Party. With the slogan of "the status is not an issue," they won the 1924 election.

Soon after the election, Muñoz left for New York, where he lived with his family for two years. Then Barceló offered him a position as director of *La Democracia.*

Muna didn't trust Barceló. Once she told Muñoz, "Don't let him deceive you into believing that he wishes you well."

Yet Muñoz felt that Barceló was like a second father to him, and he didn't want to leave without Muna and the children. They moved to Puerto Rico.

La Democracia prospered under Muñoz. For the first time the family was financially secure, and Muna didn't have to work as hard. She used her free time to participate in political activities. American women had been voting since 1920, but Puerto Rican women couldn't vote yet. Muna gave speeches and wrote articles defending the right of Puerto Rican women to vote.

The family wasn't financially secure for long. The Republicans in Barceló's party gave Muñoz a hard time. They didn't like it when Muñoz wrote that the United States dominion wasn't Americanizing the Puerto Ricans, that most Puerto Ricans considered themselves Latin Americans. Those were anti-statehood remarks.

Before Barceló could fire Muñoz, he got fed up with the Republicans. Saying that "the *flamboyan* trees are giving me indigestion," he fled without his family to New York, where "the evening lights of Fifth Avenue, as agreeable as usual, are a marvelous tonic."

Two months later, Muñoz sent Muna a cable from New York. He was penniless. His $500 salary from *La Democracia* and the extra $100 he had received from his articles were gone. Muna answered:

> I know you have had a very difficult two months. So have I. *La Democracia* has not paid Mamá anything so far this month. . . . I can't help you in any financial way but I shall be utterly lost and undone if you cannot manage to help us immediately. Believe me, our need is desperate, or I should not beg for money—and continue to beg. . . .
>
> We cannot help you, Luis. I don't know how you can arrange to help us, but you must.

Luis Muñoz Marín loved his children. But at the time he wasn't very responsible with money. He had $3.80 left in his checking account. Muna found a job as director of the Bureau of International Relations at the University of Puerto Rico. She supported the children, but didn't send Muñoz money.

He tried making money the only way he knew how—writing. He wrote essays for the most highly respected U.S. magazines. In the *American Mercury*, he described Puerto Rico as a "land of beggars and millionaires." Then, to help the American readers understand Puerto Rico's needs, he wrote in *The Nation*:

> Out of the island's total area of 2,000,000 acres, one-third is in the hands of less than 500 owners, and the soil whose ownership is so fantastically concentrated is called upon to support a population that exceeds 400 per square mile. The mass of Puerto Ricans are landless and must hire themselves out for wages that seldom rise to a dollar a day during a busy season and often fall as low as forty cents.

With the little money he made out of his writing, Muñoz bought a beat-up Ford and traveled across the nation. He found that many areas of the United States were poor. The United States had not helped Puerto Rico much before, and now it could help less. Muñoz felt that Puerto Rico had to pull itself out of its misery by its own efforts. Independence was the only choice for the island.

Back in New York, he borrowed money from his friends and, leaving the keys inside his beat-up Ford, left for Puerto Rico.

The Best Eyes in the World

1931–1937

For the stars,
For the wind, for the flowers, for the sea,
For the people,
For all the things below the stars,
All praise be to God.
For the fact that all these are good to me,
All be praise to you.

As soon as Muñoz arrived in Puerto Rico, he told his friends he favored independence as the only choice for the island.

Puerto Rico was in a depression made worse by disaster. The winds of the hurricane San Felipe had wiped out most of the coffee plants. The industry was dying, leaving hundreds of *jíbaros* jobless. Yet the *jíbaro* population was growing. In 1920, the population of Puerto Rico had been 1,299,809. That number had now jumped up to 1,543,913, and 72 percent of the population lived in rural areas.

As if blown there by the hurricane, some *jíbaros* came from the

A Puerto Rican family in El Fanguito, a smelly slum of San Juan. Today this area is a public park and people tour its clear waters.

hills seeking jobs in the city and rested in the San Juan slums of La Perla and El Fanguito. There were not many jobs for them in San Juan, either. In the evenings, fathers and children walked the streets calling, "Leftovers for our pigs!" The slop was really for their families to eat.

And the politicians? Iglesias had turned his back on the *jíbaros*. He was now more interested in getting into power, and he let his Republican backers buy votes. Barceló's Unionist-Republican Alliance Party was growing weaker. It didn't take long for the Republicans in his party to recognize that "the status" actually was an issue for them. Most of them joined Iglesias's Socialist-Republican Party, where everybody believed in statehood. Pedro Albizu Campos, president of the Nationalist Party, was the only one left talking about independence to solve the problem of poverty.

Albizu Campos was a black Puerto Rican who had studied law at Harvard University. He had suffered discrimination while serving in the U.S. Army and now thought that the Americans were the enemy. He saw his Nationalist Party as an army that would drive out the American invaders by force if necessary.

"In 1931," Muñoz later said, "Albizu visited me occasionally. We met in the mornings in my room at the Palace Hotel. He impressed me with his substance, his emotion, his passion for independence."

Nevertheless, Luis Muñoz Marín and Albizu had different styles. Muñoz wanted independence and social changes. But he thought he could accomplish all that with votes, not arms. And he didn't see the United States as the enemy.

In 1932, Antonio Barceló separated himself from the dying Unionist-Republican Alliance Party. He still wanted independence and needed the Muñoz name to succeed. So he put together Luis Muñoz Marín's ideas of social-economic justice and independence and founded what Muñoz was looking for: the Liberal Party.

For years, Muñoz had put all his creativity into writing poems and essays that spoke of justice. Now, he thought, it was time for him to create social programs and make sure justice was done. To do so, he had to become a politician. He joined the Liberal Party and campaigned with Barceló.

Muñoz said of these days: "The world of politics captured my imagination totally when I associated it with justice and creativity, which are, after all, functions of poetry . . . of the poetry you don't write because you use all its energy living it."

The political personality that had been growing in Muñoz since his socialist years began to show. He spoke of land, food, schools, hospitals, and all the other goals he had learned from Iglesias. Muñoz's deep voice, casual style, and simple language invited people to listen. Many Puerto Ricans began to believe in him.

The Socialist-Republican Party won the 1932 election, and Santiago Iglesias became the resident commissioner. Nevertheless, the Liberal Party won enough votes to send Luis Muñoz Marín to the Puerto Rican Senate.

The same day that Muñoz won his position as senator, Franklin

On this Liberal Party propaganda piece, Luis Muñoz Rivera (center) was used as a link between Luis Muñoz Marín and Antonio Barceló.

D. Roosevelt won the presidential election in the United States. Eleanor Roosevelt became the First Lady and the "President's legs." Her husband had had polio and was in a wheelchair. He depended on Mrs. Roosevelt to visit areas in need and inform him.

Ruby Black, a reporter for *La Democracia* and other well-known U.S. newspapers, wanted Mrs. Roosevelt to see Puerto Rico's needs. On one occasion when Muñoz was in Washington, D.C., she arranged for Mrs. Roosevelt to meet him. The meeting went well, and Muñoz invited Mrs. Roosevelt to visit Puerto Rico.

Five months later, Muñoz welcomed Mrs. Roosevelt, Ruby Black, and other reporters to El Morro and La Fortaleza, where the governor had his offices. Then they traveled toward the ghetto El Fanguito.

Muñoz's understanding of the American culture, his ability to speak English without an accent, and his talent with words helped him on this occasion.

"I told her that she had the best eyes in the world," he said in his autobiography. He wasn't just flattering Mrs. Roosevelt. He thought she had clear, deep, caring eyes—eyes that could see Puerto Rico's needs. He knew her heart would be touched when she saw the many residents at El Fanguito. Just before the 1932 election, another hurricane had brought more destruction to the island. And since then more *jíbaros* had moved to El Fanguito. They built their houses in the only place they were allowed to build—on a lagoon. They had no running water, and their toilet was the lagoon itself. Ruby Black wrote:

> To the great distress of the American colony in San Juan, who wanted to make Puerto Rico a rich man's playground, Mrs. Roosevelt took reporters and photographers across rickety catwalks over a dank swamp to little houses built

out of debris from the 1932 hurricane, took them to muddy alleys in sight of the beautiful Spanish palaces of the Governor and the Commandant of the 65th Infantry, stepped over pigs and game cocks into six-by-nine-foot shacks in which the poor and jobless lived and died of tuberculosis and malnutrition.

Stories and photos of Mrs. Roosevelt's visit were published in the most prominent newspapers in both Puerto Rico and the United States. The rich American growers and the past and present American governors of Puerto Rico who had done little for the island were outraged. Some dared to say they didn't know conditions were that bad, though it was all right in front of their eyes.

Eleanor Roosevelt did have "the best eyes in the world." She saw the poverty in Puerto Rico and told President Roosevelt. The President included Puerto Rico in his New Deal, a plan to help the United States recover from its Depression. Food was given to the hungry *jíbaros*. New roads, hospitals, and schools were built.

Muñoz was grateful to Ruby Black, Eleanor Roosevelt, President Roosevelt, and the United States. And most Puerto Ricans were grateful to Muñoz. He became a popular and powerful leader. Under the New Deal, he designed an economic reconstruction plan for Puerto Rico. It created jobs by constructing public housing, modernizing old buildings, clearing the slums, and building small factories. But Muñoz couldn't put his whole plan into practice.

Two men shot the San Juan chief of police, Francis Riggs, as he came out from church on February 23, 1936. "He died with his prayer book in his hand," Muñoz said, outraged. "He was my friend. He was cordial and had a good sense of humor. He had many friends, among them Albizu Campos. . . ."

The police captured the killers. They were two radicals, followers

Mrs. Eleanor Roosevelt (at the foot of the stairs) visits a Puerto Rican home in March 1934.

of the Nationalist Albizu Campos. And the police killed them without a trial. An American official, Ernest Gruening, called on Muñoz to ask him to condemn publicly the Riggs killing. Muñoz refused. He didn't approve of the Nationalists' behavior, but he also didn't like that the Nationalists were put to death without a trial.

In Washington, Senator Millard Tydings of Maryland, who had been a close friend of the chief of police, heard of Muñoz's answer. Tydings was furious and he offered a bill to grant Puerto Rico immediate independence.

Muñoz urged the Liberals to boycott the 1936 elections in protest. Political independence with economic independence now that Puerto Rico had the chance to get out of its poverty was not wise.

"The Tydings bill is not an independence bill," he said. "It is *Ley de Fuga*." Muñoz was comparing the bill to an old law under which the police used to arrest someone, tell him kindly to take off, and then shoot him in the back. "I do not want independence under the threat of starvation. I want independence with economic guarantees that will allow Puerto Ricans to survive with dignity."

Barceló disagreed. "Let independence come even if we die of hunger!" He and others saw Muñoz as a traitor to independence and expelled him from the Liberal Party.

The Tydings Bill didn't pass. But Muñoz didn't have anything to do with the decision. Congress, instead of taking such a drastic action, appointed economist Benjamin Dorfman to assess the situation of Puerto Rico.

¡Jalda Arriba!

~~~~~~

1937–1940

God, working with the stars
(His silence is profound)

The crowd stopped cheering for Luis Muñoz Marín. Many Puerto Ricans said, "He smelled like a dead body." "He was a man without a party." "He was a traitor to independence."

Antonio Barceló and his family didn't want to hear Muñoz's name. Barceló's wife even refused to let Muñoz see her husband when Barceló was dying. "Tell that man not to dare set foot in this house," she said. Barceló died without seeing Muñoz.

For a while Muñoz felt lost. But he could not rest until the *jíbaros* got enough help to get out of their extreme poverty. He felt he had to go ahead and start all over.

By himself, Muñoz knew, he couldn't do much. He had always been a man of many friends. Some were members of the Liberal Party. Others were members of the Nationalist Party. They were highly educated leaders, and they were ready for new ideas.

Muñoz gathered them and shared his thoughts. Together they founded the Popular Democratic Party.

Muñoz asked his friend Antonio Colorado to design the flag for the party. On a piece of white cloth, Colorado sketched in red the face of a *jíbaro* wearing his broad-brimmed straw hat. Underneath the portrait, Muñoz wrote: BREAD, LAND, AND LIBERTY.

The Popular Democratic Party was not going to buy votes. Muñoz Marín was determined that the *jíbaros* were going to exercise their right to vote in a democratic way. "The status" was not going to be an issue—at least not for now. The *jíbaros* didn't care if Puerto Rico was independent, autonomous, or a state. They worried about land, food, and shelter. For Muñoz Marín, the social and economic changes had to come first. Minimum wages; agricultural cooperatives; promotion of new industries; slum clearance; a food commission; a water supply program; and social security to provide assistance in unemployment, disability, old age, maternity, and sickness were some principal items on his agenda.

These were not new ideas. At one time or another, they had been in the minds of Luis Muñoz Rivera, Antonio Barceló, and Santiago Iglesias. But it took the creative mind of a poet to put them together.

Muñoz drove with his friends—"*¡Jalda arriba!*" "Up the hill!"—to Barranquitas. By his father's tomb, he said, "Luis Muñoz Rivera, we offer you a country of men who can now stand straight . . . , a country the way you wanted it to be, the way you dreamed it. . . ."

He began his campaign speaking to the *jíbaros*. "Write on a piece of paper or board whatever I promise you," he told them. "If you don't know how to write, ask one of your children or neighbors to help you. After the elections, you or somebody who knows how to read can see what is written on that piece of paper. If you can see that we didn't keep our promises, vote against us in the next election."

Puerto Ricans carry the Popular Democratic Party's flag at a rally in Ponce.

How dumb, many middle-class Puerto Ricans thought, to speak to people who couldn't read, who were not intelligent enough, who didn't even know how to vote.

Muñoz knew better. He knew that, given the opportunity, the *jíbaros* could prove themselves brighter than most politicians. He continued speaking from hillside to hillside, from footpath to footpath, telling the *jíbaros* over and over, "Don't sell your vote! If you sell your vote, you sell your sons' future. You sell the opportunity to improve your life and that of your children."

When the announcement for the first rally in San Juan came out, Muñoz's political opponents said, "Only four cats will go to that rally."

Then, when thousands of people attended, the same politicians said, "That's not an indicator of the strength of the party."

Many of those people went to the rally because they were curious or because they wanted to hear the son of Muñoz Rivera speak. Muñoz wanted these people to go to his rallies. He hoped to persuade them.

At this San Juan rally, a pro-independence man asked him, "If the Popular Democratic Party wins, what would you do to get independence?"

"Whether Puerto Rico would be independent or a state is not an issue in this election," Muñoz told him. "The votes would not be counted for or against any political status. The votes would be counted in favor of the economic-social program of the party to help the people of Puerto Rico."

The man lowered his eyes and left.

"And I," Muñoz wrote in his autobiography, "who believed in independence, understood the desolation of his spirit."

He felt tempted to bring up the issue of independence. Yet this was no time to be talking about "the status" but about bread and land that could give the *jíbaros* liberty.

More and more Puerto Ricans began to agree with Muñoz. Actually, putting off settling "the status" attracted many pro-independence Puerto Ricans to the party. They believed that once the serious economic problems were solved, Muñoz would move toward independence.

Language Is the Breath of the Spirit

ZZZZZZZZZZZZZZZZZZZZZZZZZZZZZZZZZZZZZZZZZZZZ

1937–1940

I walked today in the forest,
my love, my love;
I walked today in your heart.

Muñoz Marín had heard about Doña Inés Mendoza. She was a teacher fired because she was against the American-imposed ruling that all students must be taught in English.

"I cannot teach *Don Quijote* without teaching liberty," Doña Inés Mendoza told Muñoz when they met at a political rally during the Popular Democratic Party's first campaign.

Liberty for her was independence for Puerto Rico and for Puerto Ricans to be able to learn in Spanish.

Muñoz agreed. "A second language can enrich a country," he used to say. "But to substitute one language for another is to diminish that country's capacity to be happy."

The United States complained about the high rate of illiteracy in Puerto Rico. But teachers taught Puerto Rican children to learn to read in English. At the time, educators didn't know that people should learn to read in their native language. Although this was not the only cause of illiteracy in Puerto Rico, it didn't help.

Instead of learning English, more and more Puerto Ricans were speaking "Spanglish," a mixture of Spanish and English. Some people said "roquedora" instead of "rocking chair" or "*sillón*," and "roofo" instead of "roof" or "*techo*." Spanglish signs were seen everywhere on the island: "Laundry *aquí*!" "Agapito's Bar." "Baseball *Hoy*."

"Our language is the breath of our spirit," Muñoz said. "We shouldn't make that breath asthmatic."

Doña Inés shared Muñoz's views on language and his love for the *jíbaros*. Her father was an illiterate *jíbaro*. Once she said, "I could not have known who Muñoz was if I had not known my father. . . . [My father] bought many books and my mother read them to him. . . . He valued human beings above all else . . . and he was very humble."

Some Puerto Rican children could read English aloud, but many of them couldn't understand what they were reading.

Doña Inés had been a Nationalist and an ardent fighter for independence. But Muñoz's peaceful revolution and his urge to free the *jíbaros* from hunger before liberating the island from the United States attracted her. She began to campaign with him.

One night, Muñoz looked down from the top of a mountain and told Doña Inés, "I wonder how many people are in that darkness who have placed their hopes on me, but are unaware of it."

Doña Inés understood. Muñoz had the same hopes for the *jíbaros* that the *jíbaros* had for themselves. But many had not met him yet. Together, Doña Inés and Muñoz campaigned harder—day and night, weekdays and weekends. Together, they embraced the beauty they found in the *jíbaros*, mountains, and trees.

In 1938, Muñoz asked Doña Inés to stay with him all his life, and she accepted. Although he and Muna had been separated, he didn't divorce her until 1946 and didn't marry Doña Inés until 1947. Puerto Ricans criticized Muñoz harshly for this. In his autobiography he says: "Difficulties with the divorce explain the difference in dates. None of that has been explained publicly, although it is in the official documents. Muna was a woman of excellent quality, good, intelligent, loyal. The initiative to divorce was mine."

In Muñoz's life, Muna represented poetry and freedom. Doña Inés represented stability and Puerto Rico. In 1938, not only was Muñoz in love with Doña Inés, but he had definitely drowned his poet dreams and sought liberty not for himself but for the *jíbaros*. He was now determined to stay on the island. He and Doña Inés moved to a farm called "Treasure Island" in the town of Cidras. A year later, Viviana Muñoz Mendoza was born.

Also around this time, Luis Muñoz Lee decided to go to college. Muñoz Marín needed every penny he had for his campaign. But, encouraged by Doña Inés, he gave his son what were probably his only savings, $500, to study journalism.

When Doña Inés campaigned with Muñoz in the countryside, the jíbaras *invited her to their homes. She's sitting here on a chair made in Puerto Rico, as were the furniture and crafts she purchased for her own home.*

Doña Inés was also a strong advocate for women's rights. She encouraged Muñoz to speak to the *jíbaras*, the peasant women.

Puerto Rican women who could read and write had been voting since 1932. The illiterate women began to vote in 1936. But most politicians didn't take their votes seriously. They didn't go after the woman's vote.

In Puerto Rican society, a woman with strong opinions was not considered feminine. For that reason, she let her husband be the one to "wear the pants," be the boss, at least in public. In the privacy of their house she advised her husband and sons.

Were the *jíbaras* that strong? Muñoz felt he had to try to see. He sat at his desk and wrote:

> It is up to the mothers to tell their sons not to sell their votes. . . . It is up to the daughters to tell their fathers that they have to act like men and not like sheep for sale. It is up to the girlfriends to tell their boyfriends that they can't love men who are going to sell the future of their children for some miserable dollars that they receive one day every four years. . . .

As a result of this article and others published in *El Batey*, thousands of women joined Muñoz's campaign, and their men followed.

El Batey was the Popular Democratic Party's newspaper. It was read to illiterates, and many *jíbaros* learned to read with it. The newspaper had a circulation of 100,000 copies. Muñoz was able to fund it through advertisements purchased by the political opposition. Republican, Socialist, and Liberal businessmen viewed *El Batey* as an excellent paper in which to advertise. They didn't see any danger in supporting it because, they believed, Muñoz and his Popular Democratic Party had no chance to win.

Counting Begins with One

1937–1940

A miraculous breach had been opened in the hills
And my eyes have been released into an infinite
Vista of quiet silver.

During the first campaign, the Popular Democratic Party leaders collected a few pennies only to buy gas to drive from town to town. Sometimes they didn't even have that money. Muñoz often gave the money away to sick *jíbaros*; once, to an old lady who had lost her house in a fire.

Whenever they ran out of gas and money, the *jíbaros* invited them to stay at their houses. Muñoz ate codfish and drank coffee with the *jíbaro* families. He slept on their cots or hammocks or on the dirt floor. Feeling at home among the *jíbaros*, he explained what the problems of Puerto Rico were and their responsibilities as voters.

Sometimes Muñoz left the mountains to go to the cities and talk to the teachers and workers who hoped to get better wages. Muñoz worried every time he left his country people. His cousin, Moncho Marín, kept warning him that the *jíbaros* were going to sell their votes. If he didn't keep talking to them, another party could come and persuade them. Yet how could he be in two places at once?

Muñoz's friend Manuel Seoane solved the problem. On horseback, Manuel carried a record player to those mountains where there were no roads. Around nine in the evening, Manuel began to play the Popular Democratic Party's song, " 'Up the Hill!' Sings the Popular." Then he played one of Muñoz's speeches.

The *jíbaros* had no lanterns, and candles were too expensive for them to waste. "But as soon as the speech began," Muñoz said in

Luis Muñoz Marín speaks to a small group of jíbaros, *as was his habit in all his campaigns.*

his autobiography, "small points of candlelight appeared in the dark, to show Seoane that they were listening. It looked as if the earth were a sky full of small stars."

Manuel's method was also useful for reaching those *jíbaros* who were too scared to go to a political rally and be seen by their landowners. They were so fearful that once, when Muñoz was scheduled to speak close to a landowner's field, only one *jíbaro* showed up.

"Gather more people," Muñoz told him.

"Speak to me!" the *jíbaro* said.

"You are only one."

"Don't forget, you start counting with one."

Muñoz spoke to that one man. He told him that if the Popular Democratic Party won, the *jíbaros* could stop fearing the landowners. The *jíbaros* would own their own land!

Muñoz used to say that he taught the *jíbaros* a little bit but that they taught him more. "When I walked through the countryside, people thought I was campaigning among them. The deeper truth is that they were campaigning within me."

A few days before the election, Muñoz spoke in Barranquitas. "The word of the Popular Democratic Party is your word of faith!" he told the *jíbaros*. "Believe in yourselves. Do not believe that you are small or weak or inferior. . . . Have faith in your strength and your power to make justice and assure your future. . . . Believe in your united power to end the pain that has oppressed you. . . . Believe and have faith in democracy that is the government you have chosen. . . . Be men and women as God wanted you to be!"

He didn't visit any more towns. The day before the election, he spoke on the radio. "You need to go to vote, even if it rains. Go in silence, without allowing anyone to provoke your anger and without provoking anybody's anger. . . ."

Then Muñoz returned to the Party's headquarters in San Juan

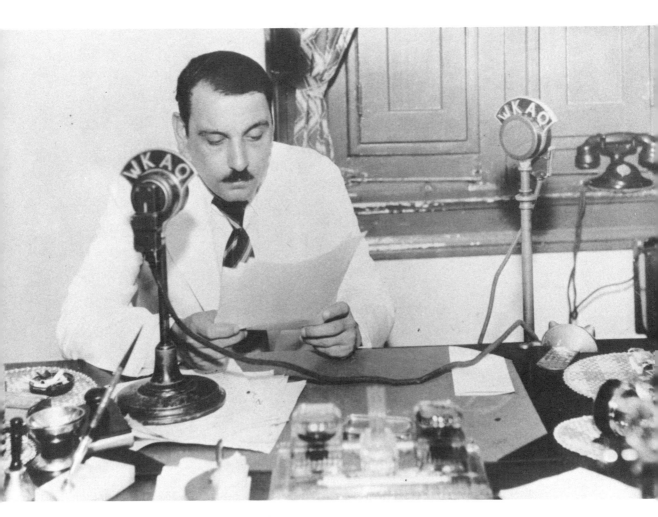

Muñoz speaks on WKAQ radio.

and stayed there overnight. It was too late to return to Treasure Island.

The next morning the telephones at the Popular Democratic Party's headquarters woke Muñoz. The calls were from people complaining about landowners who were trying to lock voters in their homes. There were rumors of politicians planning parties to get the

Don Luis writes on a rustic desk at Treasure Island. Muñoz had simple tastes.

jíbaros drunk so they couldn't vote or so they could easily be persuaded to sell their votes.

Moncho Marín had assured him that, at the end, the *jíbaros* were going to sell their votes. Muñoz wasn't sure he could win, though he had faith in the *jíbaros*. If the *jíbaros* were getting locked in, there was nothing he could do. He went to vote and returned to the party headquarters.

Later, the radio announced the early returns. The Popular Democratic Party won Bayamón, a Republican town. Muñoz did not expect to win Bayamón. Returns came from Coamo, another Republican stronghold. The party won there, too. It was winning mountain town after mountain town—Barranquitas, Villalba, Comerío. . . .

"Moncho!" Muñoz said to his cousin. "The *jíbaros* didn't sell their votes! Kneel, Moncho, kneel and apologize to God for your lack of faith in the *jíbaros*."

Other party workers burst into the office, shouting with excitement. They listened all night. By dawn all the results were in.

The pro-statehood coalition of Socialists, Republicans, and now some Liberals polled 224,423 votes. They elected nine senators and eighteen representatives. The Democrats received only 214,857 votes but elected ten senators and eighteen representatives. Three other representatives were elected by a party called Unification, composed mostly of Liberals. By winning the Senate, the Popular Democratic Party had won the presidency of the Senate and had captured the political leadership of Puerto Rico.

The victory of the Popular Democratic Party was not a landslide, but it was a triumph.

Eleven days later, Luis Muñoz Marín delivered his acceptance speech as president of the Senate. "On November sixth," he said, "Puerto Rico awoke to freedom. . . . The teachers . . . the university professors . . . the public employees . . . the farmers, all the workers of Puerto Rico awoke to freedom. . . . You don't owe this liberty to me. You owe it to the hungry men and women who came down the mountain . . . without even a cup of coffee . . . with newborns on their arms. . . . They—those simple, brave men and women—have set me free as well. . . . Puerto Rico has spoken democratically. The sun of November sixth arose burning the ropes and melting the chains of our slavery!"

Teaching Men to Fish

▚▚▚

1940–1950

A burro, climbing the mountain, slowly . . .
(His optimistic ears pointing toward the summit.)

On Christmas Eve, a month after the Popular Democratic Party won, Doña Inés gave birth to a girl. They named her Victoria, for victory.

After the election Muñoz got busy, figuring out how he could give the *jíbaros* what he had promised: bread, land, and liberty. He began an economic reform program called Operation Bootstrap. It meant that Puerto Ricans would reach down and pull themselves up by their bootstraps, up and out of trouble through their own efforts, by using available resources and making the most out of them. For them to do so, the government bought sugar, coffee, and tobacco plantations and gave jobs and land to the *jíbaros*.

That was not enough. "Give a man a fish," Muñoz said, "and he will have a single meal. Teach him to fish and he can eat the rest of his life." He wanted every Puerto Rican to be educated. He sent

Many Puerto Ricans found work with Operation Bootstrap.

social workers into the towns to recruit *jíbaros* who were interested in learning. Then, with the cooperation of businesses and schools, he offered the *jíbaros* literacy classes in Spanish and training for skills that could prepare them for jobs.

Pedro Galarza, a *jíbaro* who was so poor he was always barefoot, was interested in the program. A social worker suggested the courses the government was offering other uneducated *jíbaros*—electricity, mechanics, plumbing—but Galarza wanted to be a secretary. Encouraged by Muñoz, who said that "an ambitious man cannot be wasted," the social worker found a school for Galarza. And the government paid for his studies. After graduation, the *jíbaro* found a job as a lawyer's secretary. Then he was recommended for a job with the government. Pedro Galarza was promoted many times. Eventually he became the director of the Housing Department of Puerto Rico.

But Galarza was only one *jíbaro*. "It's not enough to share a loaf of bread among twenty people," Luis Muñoz Marín said. "More bread has to be produced to satisfy the hunger of those twenty people."

What Muñoz had done was a good start, but hunger, illiteracy,

Land was distributed among the jíbaros *by drawing numbers out of a hat.*

and overpopulation did not disappear overnight. The economic and social reform program of the Popular Democratic Party was building schools and teaching skills to the *jíbaros*. The party had acquired more than half of the American growers' land and resettled thousands of families. But the continuing increase in population minimized these dramatic gains. Although Muñoz stressed throughout his life the importance of agriculture, he also thought Puerto Rico needed industries to produce more jobs.

World War II helped Muñoz. Puerto Ricans were drafted, which eased the overpopulation. And the United States established military bases on the island, creating jobs.

Many Puerto Ricans died in the war, and many others came back wounded. Most served the United States with pride and loyalty. Muñoz, who knew how to talk to the United States, pointed this out to its leaders. They responded by offering tax incentives to Americans who opened industries in Puerto Rico. When the war ended and the soldiers returned, more than two thousand factories had jobs available. Every worker received a decent salary, and many families lived on two salaries. As veterans, the soldiers could also go to school at a reduced cost.

Muñoz built a system of scholarships and low-interest educational loans for women and men who didn't go to the war. Puerto Ricans were encouraged to go to college. Teachers had better salaries. Tourism grew, and the new hotels hired hundreds of Puerto Ricans.

The residents of the lagoon of El Fanguito began to move into the public housing built by Muñoz and his government. Some people who lived in La Perla, however, preferred to stay in their ghetto because there they owned a piece of land. Free health clinics were available for all. The *jíbaros* continued to get land to cultivate, and architects were designing houses to replace their shacks.

"Men, including you, Muñoz," Doña Inés said when she saw the

From left to right, Victoria, Doña Inés, Viviana, and Muñoz set up a nativity scene. Doña Inés used to say that Muñoz was a better father to his country than to his children, but he did find time for them.

house plans, "expect food to be ready for them. They don't even consider that women cannot cook in a three-by-six-foot kitchen. That's a hallway, not a kitchen."

The men had made a mistake. They admitted it, but then they argued that there was not enough money to buy cement to build larger kitchens. Up to now, the countryside kitchens had been outside, away from the house. They didn't have to build kitchens out of cement if they were outside.

"That's why the *jíbaras* get so many colds!" Doña Inés said. "They have to run out of the house three times a day to cook. Then, with their bodies warm from the fire, sometimes they have to run back in the rain to feed their husbands."

Doña Inés was right, the men concluded. But there was still the question of money to buy the cement.

"Why don't we ask Luis Ferré to sell us the cement for seventy-five cents a sack instead of ninety-five cents?" Muñoz asked.

"Ask Ferré?" one of the men said.

Don Luis Ferré was the chief administrator of Ponce Cement and a strong Republican leader.

"Luis Ferré is a good person," Muñoz said. "He believes statehood is the right status for Puerto Rico, but he's not a bad person."

Luis Ferré sold the cement to Muñoz at seventy-five cents a sack. And the *jíbaras* got six-by-six-foot kitchens inside their houses.

In 1947, President Truman passed the Elective Governors Act, which said Puerto Rico could elect its own governor. Two years later, Don Luis Muñoz Marín became the first elected governor of Puerto Rico.

A year after his election, a *jíbaro* named Andrés Pinto visited him. This *jíbaro*'s son had tuberculosis, and the doctor had put him on a diet of eggs and milk. Pinto couldn't afford this food unless Muñoz got him a job as a farm worker. Muñoz said he would arrange for Pinto to have the job, but then forgot. Andrés Pinto had to come back to remind him. Muñoz apologized, and a few days later went to visit the *jíbaro* with the papers to start working. Then Muñoz learned that in the meantime Andrés Pinto had explained to his neighbors why they had to vote for Muñoz and the Popular Democratic Party.

"Andrés," Muñoz asked Pinto, "how could you vote for me and keep defending me if I didn't keep my promise to you?"

Pinto didn't hesitate to answer. "It is true that you didn't keep your word to me. But I was only one. What about the rest?"

Muñoz did keep most of his economic and social reform promises. Puerto Ricans had so much faith in his word that it became popular to promise something by saying, "I seal my promise with the mustache of Don Luis Muñoz Marín."

Puerto Rico, Commonwealth of the United States

1945–1964

There is . . . a man in tatters, dirty,
Of enormous, stubborn features,
Of rude, bent muscles, like the trees,
Scrubbing his eyes avidly
With a couple of apples.

From its beginnings, the Popular Democratic Party had had two wings: one that favored autonomy and one that had believed that, once the economic problems were solved, Muñoz would move toward independence. Illiteracy was now almost nonexistent, and Puerto Rico was practically out of its extreme poverty. But the island was still a colony.

Some Populares were saying that if the Popular Democratic Party didn't try to get independence, they would form a Puerto Rican independence party. So Muñoz felt the pressure to do something about "the status."

Years before, the United States had appointed Benjamin Dorfman to assess the Puerto Rican situation. Because of the war, Dorfman didn't finish the study until 1945. Muñoz read it then, pacing the dining room with long, fast steps. From time to time, he snorted like a fenced bull. The report said that political colonialism was Puerto Rico's only reality. If the island became a state, it would have to be treated like any other state and, therefore, would have to pay federal taxes and speak English. If the island became independent, its ever-growing population would have a gloomy future without enough resources.

Muñoz had to admit it. The report was accurate. He sat at the dining table, hid his face in his hands, and cried—until he drowned another of his dreams: independence for Puerto Rico.

The next few days were hard for Muñoz. He met with his government officials and his supporters and explained his dilemma. They discussed a new status for the island, one where there was no independence and no statehood. They needed an in-between solution that would move them away from colonialism.

What about the Free Associate State that Antonio Barceló had proposed years before? That way Puerto Rico could still be linked to the United States and could have its own constitution. Many years ago, when Barceló had proposed this form of autonomy, Muñoz had not thought of it as a "serious solution." But now he saw no choice, and he made it his proposal.

In Spanish they called this new political status *Estado Libre Asociado*, which is a direct translation of the "Free Associate State." But in English they called it a "Commonwealth of the United States." They changed the name to ease the fears of any congressman who could think that they were asking for statehood or independence.

Muñoz took the idea to Washington, D.C. Carefully he and the congressmen drew up an agreement. Both sides compromised. As a Commonwealth, Puerto Rico would continue its close ties with the United States, but it would have its own constitution.

Most Populares saw the agreement as the only way they could have liberty without being slaves of hunger. But some pro-independence Populares saw it as camouflaged colonialism. They argued about it with Muñoz, and, in response, he expelled them from the party. He couldn't keep anybody in who put "the status" before the well-being of the people. That group of Populares and a few others founded the Puerto Rican Independence Party. Other Populares were ambivalent, but they stayed loyal to Muñoz and his party.

Then there was Albizu Campos. He and about three hundred other Nationalists were determined to stop Muñoz and the United States from signing the agreement.

On October 30, 1950, five followers of Albizu attacked La Fortaleza. Two policemen were wounded, and four of the radicals killed. Muñoz and his family didn't get hurt in the attack. A month later, Albizu's followers attacked again. This time the attempt was against President Harry Truman. The President himself didn't get hurt, but Muñoz was indignant. He arrested Albizu Campos, called President Truman to express his solidarity, and spoke coast to coast on the radio to the American people, condemning the crime. As a result, more Puerto Ricans and the American people supported him.

The Commonwealth agreement was submitted to referendum on June 4, 1951. The Puerto Rican Independence Party boycotted the election. But 76.5 percent of those who voted approved the agreement.

On July 25, 1952, Puerto Rico became a Commonwealth of the United States. Because of the recent attacks on Muñoz and President Truman, security was tight during the inauguration.

That day, a skinny *jíbaro* dressed in balloon pants, a white shirt, and a huge straw hat came down a mountain to go to the inauguration. Three guards stopped him at the entrance, and the *jíbaro* became afraid. He said he meant no harm, but he had been invited

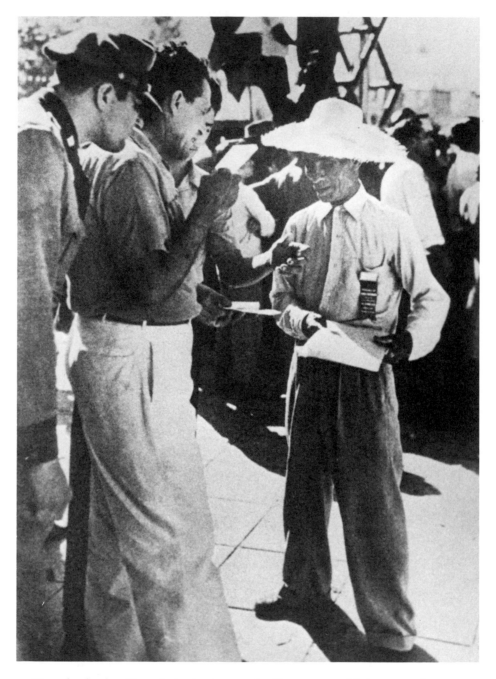

Guards check a jíbaro's invitation to the Commonwealth inauguration.

to the event. He showed the guards a personal invitation from Don Luis, and the *jíbaro* got to stay. According to Muñoz, this *jíbaro* represented Puerto Rico.

That same day, a reporter asked, "Muñoz, where do you go from here?"

And Muñoz answered, "Wait a minute. We're not there yet!"

Since Puerto Rico was not going to be independent, Muñoz feared that the *jíbaro* culture and the Spanish language could die or become more Americanized. He therefore began to encourage art and craft fairs and founded the Music Conservatory, the Pablo Casals Festival, and the Institute of Culture.

Muñoz had another problem. The new generation of *jíbaros* didn't want to plant coffee trees that the hurricanes could uproot. Nor did they want to have the seasonal work of sugarcane cutters. Instead, they wanted to work in the factories.

"The battle for a good life," Muñoz insisted, "should not have all its emphasis placed on industrialization. Part of it must be placed on agriculture."

But many *jíbaros* who wanted factory work and couldn't find any moved, usually to New York. Some American critics say that, to reduce the population, Muñoz encouraged the migration. But he was concerned. "We should not agree with this continuing situation," he said. "Our productivity also should overcome this problem." Migration continued in spite of all his efforts to create more industrial and agricultural jobs.

Even so, Don Luis was highly regarded by his people and people from around the world. President John F. Kennedy gave him the Presidential Medal of Freedom, and he received honorary degrees from Harvard and other prestigious universities.

But for Muñoz, his satisfying accomplishments were simpler: "People living in homes neither of extreme luxury nor of the slums . . . opportunity to hold an honorable job with an adequate salary

President Kennedy died before he could give Muñoz the Medal of Freedom. President Johnson gave it to Muñoz.

. . . peace of mind knowing there is education for one's children . . . security of reasonable help in times of sickness, old age, and bad luck . . . a culture of liberty, work, serenity, justice, and generosity."

He also wanted his political opponents to live and live well. Throughout his life, many of them had turned away from his views—among them Santiago Iglesias, Antonio Barceló, and Luis Ferré. But he had wished them all a good life.

One day somebody yelled, "Death to the Republicans!" Sticking his head out of his car, Don Luis yelled, "Death to nobody! Death to injustice! Death to poverty! Death to sickness! Death to the problems that oppress us! But no death to anybody who is as Puerto Rican as we are."

The Twenty-twos

ᨆᨆ

1964–1980

Yesterday, I sang of strong things—
Winds, rivers, mad slaves,
A mountain carrying me on its back to the sky,
The bosom of my beloved.

Don Luis had been governor of Puerto Rico for sixteen years in 1964 when a small group of young Populares began to insist that it was time for him to retire. They wanted the old leadership to step aside and give an opportunity to younger politicians with new ideas. They didn't want commonwealth as a permanent solution. They wanted to take the island—one step at a time—into independence.

They wrote a document asking for Muñoz's resignation and proposing that the service of elective officials be limited to two terms of four years. They made telephone calls asking people for support. There was never a formal meeting, but the telephone contacts produced twenty-two signatures. Although it never was a well-organized group, they were called "the twenty-twos."

The Twenty-twos wrote another petition to prevent Muñoz Marín from running for the position of governor. Once more, without a formal meeting, they called people, asking for support. This time they got thirty-two signatures. Among them was that of Victoria Muñoz, Don Luis's youngest daughter.

"My father didn't oppose my joining the Twenty-twos," Victoria said years later. "On the contrary!"

Muñoz believed in democracy, and in a democracy there is freedom of thought and speech. Besides, Victoria was right. To keep himself in office for too long could put democracy in danger.

The night before the Popular Democratic Party assembled to choose their candidates, Don Luis surprised everybody. He announced he was not running for governor.

"No! Four more years!" the crowd protested. "Four more!"

Don Luis explained his thinking. "Forever keep your will, your clear understanding, your good sense, your firmness of purpose. That is your strength; I am not your strength. . . . You are your own strength."

Muñoz recommended Don Roberto Sánchez Vilella for the position. The recommendation helped secure the nomination and triumph of Don Roberto as the new governor of Puerto Rico.

From 1965 to 1970, Muñoz was a senator. Nevertheless, Puerto Ricans continued to consider him the center of political power. Afraid that his opinion was too influential, the ex-governor moved with Doña Inés to Italy, where his daughter Viviana lived.

At age seventy-two, Muñoz became a European bohemian. He spent long periods in Viviana's house, but he also traveled to France, Spain, and Greece. He walked the European streets, swinging a walking cane. He wore a beret and, when it was cold, a scarf.

Doña Inés and his grandchildren traveled Europe with him. He also took his guard, Sergeant Julio Quirós. "Muñoz was a joy!" Quirós said. "He enjoyed watching the sunset from the Pantheon, going to the movies two and three times a day, drinking French and

Italian wines, and seeing people walking with loaves of bread under their arms."

Don Luis and Doña Inés spent two years in Europe and then returned to their simple house surrounded by trees in Trujillo Alto. She was always at his side. With a towel, she dried the perspiration from his forehead as he wrote his autobiography and reflected on his life.

He saw the "status" debate continuing. Three years before their trip to Europe, there had been a referendum in which 60.4 percent of the Puerto Rican voters had chosen commonwealth, 38.98 percent had voted for statehood, and 0.60 percent had supported independence.

Puerto Ricans were still proud of their language and culture. But the Republicans saw no reason why a Spanish-speaking state could

Luis Muñoz Marín with Sergeant Julio Quirós in St. Peter's Square in Rome.

not be accommodated in the increasingly multicultural society of the United States. Independence supporters insisted that Puerto Rico was a Latin American nation and as such should be on its own. Both groups saw Commonwealth as camouflaged colonialism. But most Commonwealth advocates wanted to keep the political status the way it was. In turn, Congress said it would not act until Puerto Ricans gave a clear sign of the status they wished for the island.

Muñoz thought the Commonwealth status should be made permanent. Deep in his heart he still was a supporter of independence. But the economic success of the island was now, more than ever, dependent upon the American industries.

The rural character of the Puerto Rican culture that Muñoz adored was disappearing. Few *jíbaros* had heeded his call for agriculture. The American factories had brought higher living standards. But the rapid industrialization also brought crowded neighborhoods, traffic jams, violence, pollution, and the life of the consumer. Muñoz was disappointed. He had wanted a society less attracted by material goods and more in harmony with itself and nature.

On the afternoon of January 5, 1976, he felt a pain that momentarily paralyzed his hand. He was having a stroke that left him with a quivering voice. Muñoz was a fighter. Every day he sang "Old Man River" to his grandchildren until he recovered.

Muñoz was much thinner now. He had much less hair, and what was left had turned white. He could hardly read, though he wore glasses and used a magnifying glass. He now used his cane to help him walk. Sometimes Doña Inés finished his sentences. That made him angry. He still had a good mind, even if his voice quavered.

One day, a four-year-old girl came to visit him with her parents. They met in the patio's gazebo under a straw roof. Don Luis's Italian teacher and Doña Inés joined them.

While the grown-ups talked, the girl stared at the teacher. As soon as she saw the opportunity, she asked, "Why are your teeth so big?" Everybody ignored the question and pretended they had not heard.

The girl stared at the teacher some more. A few moments later, she asked again, "Why are your teeth so big?"

Then Don Luis answered, "Because when people grow, everything grows with them, including their teeth."

The girl looked at Don Luis and asked, "Then why don't you, who are so old, have big teeth?"

"My teeth didn't grow much," Don Luis said. "But look how big my ears grew!" Don Luis flicked his huge ears. And everybody laughed.

On April 26, 1980, Don Luis developed a fever that took away all his strength. He could speak and think clearly, but he couldn't stand up without falling. Doña Inés called an ambulance. "So that you can go more comfortably to the hospital," she told him.

On April 30, Don Luis died at age eighty-two.

Until this day, his father's funeral had been the largest demonstration of sympathy in Puerto Rico. Now this was the largest. Hundreds of thousands of people of all colors, ages, social classes, and different political ideas crowded the streets and roads from San Juan to Barranquitas. The funeral car had to stop often to clear the flowers from the windshield. The trip from Aibonito to Barranquitas that normally takes fifteen minutes took five hours.

When the funeral car finally arrived at the cemetery, dozens of people rushed to the back of the hearse, pushing, shoving. They didn't mean to be disrespectful. They just wanted to carry the casket.

"Please, let's bury Muñoz with dignity!" Victoria Muñoz called out, and they moved aside.

The weight of the bodies, however, had sealed the hearse's lock, and it had to be broken. Finally the casket was taken out. Many grieving Puerto Ricans carried it to his burial.

Years later, Pedro Galarza spoke in Barranquitas. He was the

Luis Muñoz Marín's funeral procession enters Barranquitas. The sign says "Muñoz—with you—we lifted up a country."

jíbaro who became the director of the Housing Department. He said, "Muñoz gave up his poet's dreams for the dreams of those with bare feet. Mine were bare feet . . . and here, by his tomb, they are wearing shoes."

Galarza's words echoed through the mountains. Those were the words of hundreds of grateful *jíbaros*.

Afterword

Gone to feed the roots of the gathering spring.

The economic growth in Puerto Rico continued after Muñoz. But it never reached the standards of the United States.

Puerto Rico's per capita income is the highest in Latin America, but it is less than half that of the United States. Most Puerto Rican farmlands now are urbanized. The islanders depend mostly on the jobs provided by U.S. companies. Yet there are not enough such jobs for the 3.7 million people on the island. Unemployment and crime rates also are higher than those of any state. Although the literacy rate is 88 percent, public education in Puerto Rico is in a shambles, causing many parents to sacrifice and send their children to private schools.

Most Republicans believe that if Puerto Rico becomes a state, most of its social and economic problems could be solved. In 1992, they proposed a referendum to determine whether or not Puerto

Ricans wanted the island to join the Union, continue as a Common-wealth, or become an independent nation.

On November 14, 1993, almost 1.7 million voters participated in the referendum. A total of 823,859, or 48.4 percent, favored continuing as a Commonwealth, while 785,859, or 46.2 percent, favored statehood, and 75,253, or 4.4 percent, supported independence.

Most Puerto Ricans decided for commonwealth because they want to keep their culture and language while enjoying the benefits of their American citizenship. But since statehood lost by a narrow margin, the Republicans pledged to come back with another referendum in 1997.

Luis Muñoz Marín in one of his campaigns. The top sign reads "Always, up the hill."

Before the 1993 referendum, members of Congress were asked whether or not they would accept Puerto Rico in the Union. Congress chose to remain silent and wait for the referendum results. Some Puerto Ricans thought that to petition statehood and be turned down was going to be too painful for them. So they voted for commonwealth. But if in 1997 Congress gives any signal showing that it will accept Puerto Rico in the Union, statehood might win.

But would statehood solve the social and economic problems of the island?

The problems in Puerto Rico are magnified by its high population, but they are not unique to the island. Many states are struggling with high unemployment and crime rates, lack of funds for education, and thousands of homeless people on the streets—a problem that hasn't yet been as bad in Puerto Rico as it is in the United States.

So what can we do? The future will tell.

Speaking of the poor, Don Luis Muñoz Marín once said: "The great task is to unleash their creative energies. And the first great step is reached when they join together to work with enthusiasm and purpose, armed with adequate technical tools to achieve their own solution."

Then he added, "The great engines of creative energy in people are hope and pride. . . . If people cannot be given hope and pride, what is left to them? The answer is simple: despair and probably violence. . . . Only by reaching people spiritually can the necessary material tasks be undertaken successfully."

Luis Muñoz Marín took Puerto Rico out of its extreme poverty. But he did not do it alone. Even the poor, illiterate *jíbaros* were leaders then.

At a campaign rally in 1939, so many people showed up, Don Luis was afraid his words couldn't be heard at the edge of the crowd.

"The ones over there," he asked, "those under that tree, can you hear me?"

A *jíbaro* stepped forward, formed a megaphone with his hands, and answered, "We can't hear you, but we understand you. Go ahead."

"Ahead" Muñoz continued, and "ahead" we should continue, without forgetting the days when the crowd cheered, "Up with Muñoz Marín!"

And he answered, "Up with you!"

And when the crowd booed, "Down with Muñoz Marín!" he cheered, "Up with you!"

We cannot hear Luis Muñoz Marín's voice anymore, but we can still understand his message to "go with the mob of stars and hungry [people] toward the great dawn."

Appendix

^^

MAIN EVENTS

1897	Spain grants autonomy to Puerto Rico (effective February 10, 1898).
1898	February 10: Luis Muñoz Rivera becomes prime minister.
	February 18: José Luis Muñoz Marín is born.
	April 21: the Spanish-American War begins.
	July 25: American troops land in Guánica, Puerto Rico.
	December 10: Spain signs the Treaty of Paris, which cedes Puerto Rico to the United States.
1898–1900	U.S. military government in Puerto Rico.
1900	Foraker Act makes Puerto Rico a U.S. colony.
1916	November 16: Luis Muñoz Rivera dies.
1917	U.S. Congress approves the Jones Bill.
1920	Luis Muñoz Marín joins the Socialist Party.
1922	Nationalist Party is founded.
1930	Pedro Albizu Campos is elected president of the Nationalist Party.
1931	Liberal Party is founded.
1932	Luis Muñoz Marín becomes senator.
1936	Followers of Albizu Campos kill Colonel Riggs.
1937	Luis Muñoz Marín expelled from Liberal Party.
	Congress asks Benjamin Dorfman to study the case of Puerto Rico. World War II delays the report.

1938	Popular Democratic Party is founded by Luis Muñoz Marín.
1940	Popular Democratic Party wins election by narrow margin. Luis Muñoz Marín becomes president of the Senate of Puerto Rico.
1944	Popular Democratic Party wins election overwhelmingly.
1945	Dorfman's report does not recommend statehood or independence for Puerto Rico. Muñoz and his officials decide Puerto Rico should become a Commonwealth.
1946	Puerto Rican Independence Party is founded.
1947	President Truman passes Elective Governors Act.
1948	Popular Democratic Party wins the election.

Luis Muñoz Marín elected governor of Puerto Rico. |
| 1950 | July 3: President Harry S. Truman approves the Commonwealth agreement (Public Law 600).

October 30: Nationalist attempt against Luis Muñoz Marín.

November 2: Nationalist attempt against President Truman. |
| 1952 | July 25: the Estado Libre Asociado, known as the Commonwealth, is installed.

November: the Popular Democratic Party wins the election. |
1956	Popular Democratic Party wins the election.
1960	Popular Democratic Party wins the election.
1964	Luis Muñoz Marín retires as governor.
1967	Referendum in which 60.4 percent of the voters choose commonwealth.
1980	April 30: Luis Muñoz Marín dies.
1993	Referendum in which Puerto Ricans decide to stay as a Commonwealth, but statehood loses by a narrow margin.

WHAT IS IN A PUERTO RICAN NAME?

The clerk at Georgetown Preparatory School registered José Luis as "Rivera, Joseph Louis Muñoz." The correct way would have been "Muñoz Marín, José Luis." In Puerto Rico, as in most Latin American countries, the father's surname is followed by the mother's surname. Sometimes the mother's surname is dropped, but never in official documents.

This is the pattern:

First name   Father's surname   Mother's surname

Here are some examples in the Muñoz family:

Luis Muñoz Marín's FATHER:

Muñoz (father's surname)   Rivera (mother's surname)

Luis Muñoz Rivera

Luis Muñoz Marín's MOTHER:

Marín (father's surname)   Castilla (mother's surname)

Amalia Marín Castilla*

LUIS MUÑOZ MARÍN:

Muñoz (father's surname)   Marín (mother's surname)

Luis Muñoz Marín

*When a Puerto Rican woman marries, she replaces her mother's surname with the word *de*, meaning "of," followed by her husband's father's surname. For example, when Amalia Marín Castilla married Luis Muñoz Rivera, she became Amalia Marín de Muñoz.

OTHER ELECTED GOVERNORS OF PUERTO RICO

1964–68	Roberto Sánchez Vilella	(Popular Democratic Party)
1968–72	Luis A. Ferré	(New Progressive Party—Republican)
1972–76	Rafael Hernández Colón	(Popular Democratic Party)
1976–84	Carlos Romero Barceló	(New Progressive Party)
1984–92	Rafael Hernández Colón	(Popular Democratic Party)
1992–	Pedro Roselló*	(New Progressive Party)

* Pedro Roselló ran against Victoria Muñoz, Luis Muñoz Marín's youngest daughter. She was running for the Popular Democratic Party.

PUERTO RICAN POPULATION GROWTH

Year	Population	Annual Rate of Growth
1899	953,243	——
1910	1,118,012	1.54
1920	1,299,809	1.56
1930	1,543,013	1.69
1940	1,869,255	1.93
1950	2,210,703	1.69
1960	2,349,544	0.61*
1970	2,947,293	2.32
1980	3,634,021	2.12

* Migration to the United States helped lower the Puerto Rican population annual rate of growth from 1.69 percent in 1950 to 0.61 percent in 1960. In the 1950s, it averaged 42,083 each year, and it skyrocketed to 74,603 in 1953. Birth control education also helped. But Puerto Rico was mostly Catholic. At a mass rally on May 22, 1960, the Catholic Church censured Luis Muñoz Marín and his Popular Democratic Party for the dissemination of birth control information.

CHANGES IN THE PUERTO RICAN GOVERNMENT (1897–PRESENT)

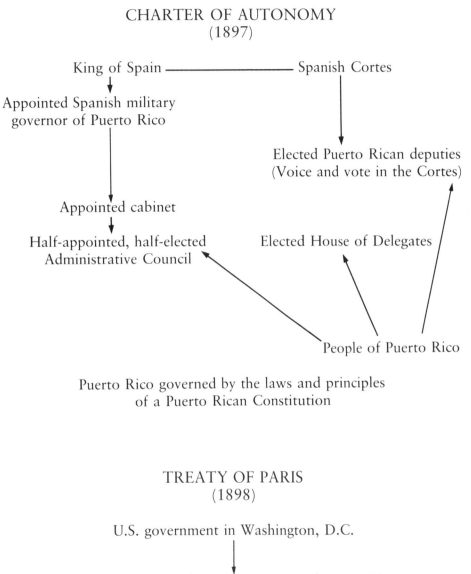

CHARTER OF AUTONOMY
(1897)

King of Spain ——————————— Spanish Cortes

Appointed Spanish military
governor of Puerto Rico

Elected Puerto Rican deputies
(Voice and vote in the Cortes)

Appointed cabinet

Half-appointed, half-elected   Elected House of Delegates
Administrative Council

People of Puerto Rico

Puerto Rico governed by the laws and principles
of a Puerto Rican Constitution

TREATY OF PARIS
(1898)

U.S. government in Washington, D.C.

Appointed U.S. military government of Puerto Rico

FORAKER ACT
(1900)

U.S. government in Washington, D.C.

Elected Puerto Rican resident
commissioner to U.S. House
(given voice but no vote in
Congress in 1904)

Appointed American civil governor of Puerto Rico

Appointed Executive Council

Elected Puerto Rican
House of Delegates

People of Puerto Rico

Puerto Rico governed by the laws and principles
of the U.S. Constitution

JONES BILL
(1917)

Appointed Executive Council replaced by elected Puerto Rican Senate
and House of Representatives

People of Puerto Rico
(U.S. citizenship and military draft)

ELECTIVE GOVERNORS ACT
(1947)

Elected Puerto Rican civil governor

People of Puerto Rico

COMMONWEALTH OF PUERTO RICO
(1952–present)

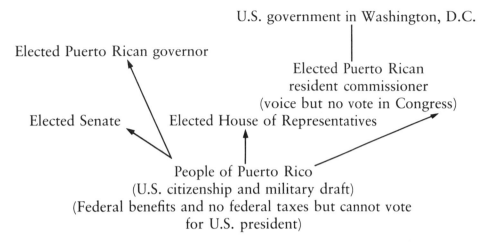

U.S. government in Washington, D.C.

Elected Puerto Rican governor

Elected Puerto Rican
resident commissioner
(voice but no vote in Congress)

Elected Senate   Elected House of Representatives

People of Puerto Rico
(U.S. citizenship and military draft)
(Federal benefits and no federal taxes but cannot vote
for U.S. president)

Puerto Rico, Commonwealth of the United States, governed by the laws
and principles of the Puerto Rican Constitution

Sources and Other Information

Unless otherwise noted, all epigraphs, quotations, letters, and details of dialogue are from one of the following sources, with translations by the author:

Luis Muñoz Marín Foundation Archives, Río Piedras

Luis Muñoz Marín, *Las memorias* (San Juan: Inter-American University Press, 1982)

Carmelo Rosario Natal, *La juventud de Luis Muñoz Marín* (Río Piedras: Editorial Edil, 1989)

AT THE BIRTH OF A NEW CENTURY (1898–1900)

p. 1, *Autonomy*: On November 25, 1897, Spain signed the Charter of Autonomy for Puerto Rico. But the autonomic cabinet in which Luis Muñoz Rivera held the post of prime minister was not installed until February 10, 1898. The cabinet consisted of five ministers and a prime minister appointed by the governor.

p. 1, *Birth*: On February 18, 1898, José Luis Alberto Muñoz Marín was born at 19 Fortaleza Street. Today stores occupy the building.

p. 1, *Newspapers*: Luis Muñoz Rivera's father-in-law, Ramón Marín, helped him start *La Democracia* in Ponce. The first issue came out on July 1, 1890. The first issue of *El Diario* came out on January 5, 1900.

p. 2, *The Spanish-American War* originated with the Cuban struggle for independence from Spain. The United States had business investments in Cuba and wanted to acquire the island, or, if that was not possible, wanted it to be independent. The U.S. sent the battleship *Maine* to protect Cuba. On February 15, 1898—three days before Luis Muñoz Marín's birth—a huge explosion destroyed the *Maine*. After that, the U.S. and Spain tried to negotiate, but they did not come to an agreement. On April 24, Spain declared war on the United States. But Spain was ill prepared. By July, Spain was asking France to help arrange peace negotiations. On December 10, 1898, the Treaty of Paris was signed. Spain granted Cuba independence, ceded Puerto Rico and Guam to the United States, and parted with the Philippines in exchange for $20 million from the U.S.

p. 4, *"Long live the Americans!"*: Everett Marshall, ed., *Exciting Experiences in Our Wars with Spain and the Filipinos* (Chicago: The Educational Company, 1900), 146.

p. 4, *Illiteracy* in Puerto Rico in 1901 was 77 percent.

p. 5, *The Foraker Act* was named for its sponsor, Senator Joseph B. Foraker of Ohio, and was passed on April 12, 1900. Under this law, a governor and his Executive Council were to be appointed by the president of the United States. There was also a House of Delegates elected by Puerto Ricans who could read and write. But the delegates were powerless. The Executive Council was dominated by Americans, and they and the American governor could reject House legislation. The only Puerto Rican representation in Congress was a resident commissioner in the U.S. House of Representatives who could observe but not vote.

p. 5, *José Celso Barbosa* (1857–1921) was Luis Muñoz Rivera's personal friend but his political adversary. Under Spanish rule, Barbosa and Luis Muñoz Rivera had traveled to Spain to ask for autonomy. But Barbosa wanted to talk only to the antimonarchy Spanish Republican Party. Luis Muñoz Rivera, on the other hand, was willing to negotiate for autonomy with any political group in Spain. Práxedes Mateo Sagasta, a Liberal-Monarchist, promised Muñoz Rivera autonomy. As soon as Sagasta became the Spanish prime minister, he granted it.

AN UPSIDE-DOWN SKY (1900–1905)

p. 7, *"Our Father . . ."*: Luis Muñoz Marín, *Our Father*.

p. 9, *"there is not such a thing as 'we' and 'them' "*: Luis Muñoz Marín, *Historia del Partido Popular Democrático* (San Juan: Editorial El Batey, 1984), 85.

p. 9, *"What is the name of that flower?"*: Enrique Bird Piñero, *Don Luis Muñoz Marín* (Río Piedras: Fundación Luis Muñoz Marín, 1991), 157.

p. 10, *"I was not born to emit the note"*: Luis Muñoz Rivera, "Adelante," *El Pueblo* (Ponce, 1882).

IF I WERE A TREE (1905–1910)

p. 11, *" . . . The green foliage"*: Luis Muñoz Marín, "Yo soy tu flauta," poem that won an award at the Floral Games celebrated May 4, 1919.

p. 12, *"I don't remember belonging to any class"*: Luis Muñoz Marín, *Historia del Partido Popular Democrático* (San Juan: Editorial El Batey, 1984), 85.

p. 14, *Muñoz daydreamed a lot*: He dreamed that he was a song composer, one of the Three Musketeers, a Greek soldier, a pirate, and Robinson Crusoe. He also dreamed of being a correspondent at *La Democracia*.

p. 14, *"I understand and I smile"*: Luis Muñoz Marín, "Yo soy tu flauta."

p. 15, *"Your son is undisciplined"*: Pedro Moczó to Luis Muñoz Rivera, in Philip Sterling and María Brau, *The Quiet Rebels* (Garden City, N.Y.: Doubleday, 1968), 94.

p. 15, *"My observations of José Luis"*: Luis Muñoz Rivera to Pedro Moczó, June 17, 1909.

JOE RIVERA (1910–1916)

p. 16, *"Tell me, umbrella-mongers"*: Luis Muñoz Marín, "Umbrella," in "Queries," *Poetry* (between October 1924 and March 1925), 136–37; *La juventud*, 177.

p. 16, *Georgetown registration*: Rector's Entrance Book: Georgetown Preparatory School, Lauinger Library, Georgetown University.

p. 16, *Porto Rico* was the name the Americans gave to the island.

p. 18, *Citizenship*: José Luis had Puerto Rican citizenship, which didn't mean anything internationally because Puerto Rico was not an independent nation.

p. 19, *From prep school to law school*: At the time, people could go to law school or medical school without having to go through college.

p. 19, *"always behaved like a poet"*: Philip Sterling and María Brau, *The Quiet Rebels* (Garden City, N.Y.: Doubleday, 1968), 94.

DEATH OF A GIANT (1916)

p. 21, " . . . *The bells toll, and toll"*: Luis Muñoz Marín, "Mi gratitud," in *Juan Bobo* (December 2, 1916).

p. 25, *"How much he loved Puerto Rico"*: "Muñoz en el tiempo," in *El Reportero* (April 30, 1982).

p. 25, *"I would like to be a giant"*: Luis Muñoz Marín, "Mi gratitud," in *Juan Bobo* (December 2, 1916).

THE BOHEMIAN POET (1916–1918)

p. 26, *"This vulgar world"*: Luis Muñoz Marín, "Canción de los cinco perros flacos," in *La juventud*, 228.

p. 26, *"A few lines"*: Amalia (Maló) Marín vda. de Muñoz Rivera to José (Pepe) Muñoz Rivera, New York, May 31, 1917.

p. 28, *Borrones* was published in 1917 by Imprenta La Democracia in San Juan, Puerto Rico.

p. 28, *"The play had been produced"*: Peggy Mann, *Luis Muñoz Marín: The Man Who Remade Puerto Rico* (New York: Coward, McCann & Geoghegan, 1976), 35.

p. 28, *"You know that girls"*: Amalia (Maló) Marín vda. de Muñoz Rivera to José (Pepe) Muñoz Rivera, New York, May 31, 1917.

p. 29, *Edwin Markham's* poem "The Man with the Hoe" was published in his book *The Man with the Hoe and Other Poems* by Edwin Markham (New York: Doubleday & McClure, 1899).

p. 29, *The Man with the Hoe*: The author chose the poem as an example of the kind of poetry Muñoz and his group discussed because it was one of Muñoz's favorites. But we don't know when Luis Muñoz Marín read "The Man with the Hoe" for the first time. He met Edwin Markham in 1918 when Markham wrote an article for Muñoz's *Revista de Indias*. Later, Muñoz Marín moved a quarter mile from Markham's house on Staten Island. "The Man with the Hoe" inspired José Luis to write poems about the *jíbaros*, but he didn't write the ones we know about until 1920.

p. 29, *Muñoz and his writer friends* called their group *Peña de La Mallorquina* (La Mallorquina Group) because most evenings they ate at La Mallorquina Restaurant. Many of them became famous: Luis Palés Matos, Evaristo Ribera Chevremont, Antonio Coll y Vidal, José Isaac de Diego Padró, Tomás Blanco, Miguel Guerra Mondragón, Luis Loréns Torres, Antonio Pérez Pierret, and Nemesio Canales. In 1918 Luis Muñoz Marín, Evaristo Ribera Chevremont, and Antonio Coll y Vidal had a fifty-page booklet of stories published. They entitled it *Madre Haraposa (Mother in Rags)*.

p. 29, *Puerto Ricans criticized José Luis*: José Luis had asked a family friend, Fano Vanga, to write the preface for *Borrones*. Vanga wrote, " . . . the title, *Ink Blots*, with which he had christened his work, is in a way modest, although in a way it is true." Other critics agreed. The book was not very good.

p. 29, *"Blessed is Puerto Rico"*: Luis Muñoz Marín in *La Democracia* (July 9, 1917).

p. 31, *"I have an honorable name"*: Luis Muñoz Marín in *La Democracia* (June 5, 1917).

NEW YORK (1918–1920)

p. 32, *"Talkative city of one-thousand dialogues"*: Luis Muñoz Marín, "New York," in *La juventud*, 72.

p. 32, *"When I knew I could [write], I knew I was a free man"*: Philip Sterling and María Brau, *The Quiet Rebels* (Garden City, N.Y.: Doubleday, 1968), 97.

p. 33, *"The thought of you is"*: Muna Lee, "The Thought of You," in *Sea Change* by Muna Lee (New York: Macmillan, 1923), 12; *La juventud*, 154.

p. 33, *"These are singing things"*: Luis Muñoz Marín, "Interpretation," in *The Smart Set* (February 1920), 67; *La juventud*, 150.

p. 33, *Muñoz's American poet friends*: Some of Muñoz's American poet friends became famous. Among them were Vachel Lindsay, Edgar Lee Masters, and Carl Sandburg.

p. 33, *"What have these men"*: Luis Muñoz Marín in *Cuasimodo* 2 (1919).

p. 35, *"You can trade literature"*: Luis Muñoz Marín to Fano Vanga (July 4, 1922).

p. 36, *Nemesio Canales*, Muñoz's friend from La Mallorquina Group, had published his magazine entitled *Cuasimodo* in Panama and wanted to do the same in Argentina.

WITH THE MOB OF HUNGRY PEOPLE (1920)

p. 37, *"Listen to us, Universe"*: Luis Muñoz Marín, "Escúchanos," in "Cantos de la humanidad forcejando," *Cuasimodo* 4 (June–July 1920).

p. 41, *The Pamphlet*: Luis Muñoz Marín in "Cantos de la humanidad forcejando," *Cuasimodo* 4.

SAND AND ASHES WERE LESS FREE (1920–1931)

p. 43, *"Beloved, do not fear"*: Luis Muñoz Marín, "Voices," in "Queries," *Poetry* (between October 1924 and March 1925), 136–37; *La juventud*, 177.

p. 43, *Iglesias's about-face*: At a meeting on October 6, 1920, Santiago Iglesias proposed that the Socialist Party join forces with the Republicans. Muñoz pointed out that the Republican Party opposed every social and economic principle for which the Socialists had fought. Iglesias argued that both parties believed in statehood. And he felt that he couldn't put in practice his social justice program unless the Unionists, who had won every election since 1904, were defeated. That day, the Socialist Party let in many Republicans.

p. 45, *Political Campaigns*, the three volumes in which Luis Muñoz Marín compiled his father's work were published in 1925.

p. 45, *Muna's argument*: Muna loved Puerto Rico, but she didn't want to follow her husband into an unstable life again. In New Jersey, Muñoz had been quiet and, although we don't know whether or not she gave Muñoz the argument about its being hard to come and go with the children, she was a good mother and it seems reasonable that she did so.

p. 45, *"I have had enough of glamour"*: Muna Lee, "I Have Had Enough of Glamour," in *Sea Change*, by Muna Lee (New York: Macmillan, 1923), 29; *La juventud*, 154.

p. 45, *"I make no question"*: Muna Lee, "Foreword," in *Sea Change*, 52; *La juventud*, 155.

p. 46, *Antonio Barceló* and the Republican leader, José Tous Soto, feared the growing strength of the coalition of Socialists and Republicans. In the 1924 election the Unionist-Republican Alliance won 163,041 to 90,479. In 1928 they again won the election, but only by 9,410 votes.

p. 46, *Muñoz and Barceló*: Some critics say that *La Democracia* was in a shambles, one of the reasons why Barceló wanted Muñoz as a director. They also say that after Muñoz Rivera's death Barceló had wanted to take advantage of Muñoz's name to win success for himself. Others say that Barceló had the best fatherly intentions for Muñoz.

p. 46, *"the* flamboyan *trees"*: Luis Muñoz Marín to Antonio Barceló, October 5, 1927.

p. 47, *"I know you have had a very difficult two months"*: Muna Lee to Luis Muñoz Marín, November 3, 1927.

p. 47, *"land of beggars"*: Luis Muñoz Marín, "The Sad Case of Puerto Rico," in *The American Mercury* 62 (1929): 158.

p. 47, *"Out of the island's total area"*: Luis Muñoz Marín, "What Is Next in Porto Rico?," in *The Nation* (November 20, 1929), 609.

p. 48, *Muñoz crossing the United States in his old Ford*: Doña Inés Mendoza, "Oíamos hablar de Muñoz," Luis Muñoz Marín Foundation Archives, booklet. This might have happened at an earlier time in the 1920s but, considering that biographer Carmelo Rosario Natal said in *La juventud* (p. 205): "between 1928 and 1931 we have little information," the author thought this may have been the time when Luis Muñoz Marín crossed the nation.

p. 48, *The United States was poor* because it was in the Great Depression, an economic crisis that left many people in the United States and other countries without jobs. It began roughly in October 1929 and continued through the 1930s.

THE BEST EYES IN THE WORLD (1931–1937)

p. 49, *"For the stars"*: Luis Muñoz Marín, "Acknowledgement," in *Present-Day American Literature* (October 1930): 18; *La juventud*, 209.

p. 51, *The Nationalist Party* was founded in 1922, but it didn't turn toward armed struggle until 1932—two years after Albizu became the party's president.

p. 53, *"To the great distress"*: Ruby Black, *Eleanor Roosevelt* (New York: Duell, Sloan and Pearce, 1940), 296.

p. 54, *Muñoz's reconstruction* program was called the Puerto Rican Reconstruction Administration (PRRA). It was headed by Muñoz's friend, Carlos Chardón.

p. 54, *Francis Riggs*: The hostilities that led to Francis Riggs's assassination began on October 24, 1935. On this occasion there was an encounter between the police and the Nationalists outside the University of Puerto Rico. Four Nationalists and one policeman were killed and about forty people were wounded. Albizu Campos said then he would be revenged, and that led to Riggs's killing. Another sad encounter was that of the "Ponce Massacre." The mayor of Ponce had given permission to the Nationalists to have a peaceful parade on March 21, 1935, Palm Sunday. But the day of the parade, Governor Blanton Winship sent the new chief of police to cancel the mayor's permit. The Nationalists said it was too late to cancel the parade and went ahead with it. A police officer stepped into the street and ordered the parade to halt. A shot rang out, followed by multiple bursts of gunfire that killed twenty people and injured more than one hundred— some of whom were innocent spectators coming out of church.

p. 55, *"The Tydings Bill is not an independence bill"*: Davey William George, "Luis Muñoz Marín: A Rhetorical Analysis of Political Economic Modernization in Puerto Rico" (Ph.D. diss., Indiana University, 1974), 96.

p. 56, *"I do not want independence"*: Philip Sterling and María Brau, *The Quiet Rebels* (Garden City, N.Y.: Doubleday, 1968), 105.

p. 56, *"Let independence come"*: Manuel Maldonado-Denis, *Puerto Rico: A Socio-Historic Interpretation* (New York: Random House, 1972), 124.

¡JALDA ARRIBA! (1937–1940)

p. 57, *Jalda* is the *jíbaro* word for *falda*, which in this case means "foot of the hill."

p. 57, *"God, working with the stars"*: Luis Muñoz Marín, "Proletarios," in "Cantos de la humanidad forcejando," *Cuasimodo* 4 (June–July 1920).

p. 57, *"He smelled like a dead body . . . a man without a party . . . a traitor to independence"*: Author's informal interviews with Puerto Rican friends and relatives.

p. 57, *"Tell that man"*: Enrique Bird Piñero, *Don Luis Muñoz Marín: El poder de la excelencia* (Río Piedras: Fundación Luis Muñoz Marín, 1991), 76.

p. 57, *Antonio Barceló's death*: Some critics claim that the deaths of Antonio Barceló in 1938 and Santiago Iglesias in 1939 helped Muñoz and the Popular Democratic Party succeed.

p. 58, *The group that began the Popular Democratic Party* had individuals with experience in government and organization. Some of those were Ernesto Ramos Antonini, Samuel Quiñones, Vicente Géigel Polanco, Jesús Piñero, Antonio Fernós Isern, and Felisa Rincón de Gautier. There was also a group of young men: Teodoro Moscoso, Antonio Colorado, Enrique del Toro, Jaime Benítez, Rafael Picó, and Roberto Sánchez Vilella.

p. 58, *"Luis Muñoz Rivera, we offer"*: Luis Muñoz Marín, July 17, 1939, speech.

p. 60, *"Only four cats"* and *"That's not an indicator"*: Luis Muñoz Marín, *Historia del Partido Popular Democrático* (San Juan: Editorial El Batey, 1984), 22.

LANGUAGE IS THE BREATH OF THE SPIRIT (1937–1940)

p. 61, *"I walked today"*: Luis Muñoz Marín, "Song," in *The Smart Set* (October 1922), 48; *La juventud*, 150.

pp. 61, 62, *"A second language"* and *"Our language is the breath of our spirit"*: Luis Muñoz Marín, "La personalidad puertorriqueña en el Estado Libre Asociado," November 29, 1953, speech.

p. 62, *"I could not have known who Muñoz was"*: Thomas Aitken, *Poet in the Fortress* (New York: New American Library, 1964), 115.

p. 63, *Separation of Muna and Muñoz*: It is hard to know when Muna and Muñoz separated for good. In 1927 he left his job at *La Democracia* and went to New York without Muna. In February 1928, however, they both went to the Sixth Pan-American Conference in Havana, Cuba. She was a speaker on women's rights and he was a translator. But then he went back to New York and she stayed working at the University of Puerto Rico. When he returned to the island in 1931, she was living with his mother and he stayed at the Hotel Palace. But later they lived together on the third floor of the building where *La Democracia* was published.

p. 63, *Muñoz was harshly criticized* for living with Doña Inés. But at the time it was common for a Puerto Rican man to have a mistress. Doña Inés was also criticized. She was married when she met Muñoz. Her husband was the graphic artist Rafael Palacios, and they had two children, Carmen and Rafael.

p. 63, *Muna representing poetry and Doña Inés representing stability* is the author's interpretation.

p. 65, *"It is up to the mothers"*: Luis Muñoz Marín, "Lean esto las mujeres de nuestros campos," *El Batey* (April 1939).

p. 65, *El Batey*: The first issue of *El Batey* came out in March 1939.

COUNTING BEGINS WITH ONE (1937–1940)

p. 66, *"A miraculous breach"*: Luis Muñoz Marín, "Two," in *The Smart Set* (February 1923), 78; *La juventud*, 151.

p. 67, *"Up the Hill"* is the theme song of the Popular Democratic Party. In Spanish, it says *"Jalda arriba—va cantando el popular."*

p. 68, *"Gather more people"*: Peggy Mann, *Luis Muñoz Marín: The Man Who Remade Puerto Rico* (New York: Coward, McCann & Geoghegan, 1976), 87.

p. 68, *"When I walked through the countryside"*: Luis Muñoz Marín, *Historia del Partido Popular Democrático* (San Juan: Editorial El Batey, 1984), 113.

p. 68, *"The word of the Popular Democratic Party"* and *"Believe in yourselves"*: Miguel Hernández Agosto, quoting Luis Muñoz Marín, "Discurso en torno al natalicio de Don Luis Muñoz Marín," February 18, 1990, speech.

p. 71, *1940 and 1944 elections*: In 1940 the Popular Democratic Party (P.D.P.) won by a narrow margin. But in 1944 it won overwhelmingly. Out of 591,978 votes cast, the P.D.P. obtained 383,280 against 101,779 for the Republicans, who came second. The P.D.P. won more seats in the Senate and House than the three other parties combined.

p. 71, *"On November sixth"*: Luis Muñoz Marín, San Juan, November 16, 1940, acceptance speech.

TEACHING MEN TO FISH (1940–1950)

p. 73, *"A burro, climbing the mountain"*: Luis Muñoz Marín, "Proletarios," in "Cantos de la humanidad forcejando," *Cuasimodo* 4 (June–July 1920).

p. 73, *"Operation Bootstrap"*: While it started in 1942, the outbreak of World War II kept its tax incentive program from getting fully under way until 1947. Under that program, the American industries do not have to pay income taxes for up to ten years on any new factory built on the island. Between 1948 and 1965, 1,027 new factories were built on the island, but even then Muñoz couldn't lower the unemployment enough because of the growth in population.

p. 73, *"Give a man a fish"*: Abbott Chrisman, *Luis Muñoz Marín* (Austin: Steck-Vaughn, 1991), 14.

p. 75, *"It's not enough to share a loaf of bread"*: Luis Muñoz Marín, July 17, 1951, speech.

p. 76, *Tourism*: In 1955, Puerto Rico had 134,625 tourists, who spent $22.9 million on the island. Ten years later, the number grew to 606,093 tourists, who spent $119.3 million.

p. 76, *Dialogue with Doña Inés*: Enrique Bird Piñero, *Don Luis Muñoz Marín: El poder de la excelencia* (Río Piedras: Fundación Luis Muñoz Marín, 1991), 202–203.

p. 78, *Don Luis Ferré* was governor of Puerto Rico from 1968 to 1972.

p. 78, *First Puerto Rican governor*: Although most of the American governors were insensitive to the needs of Puerto Rico, there were two who cared for the island—Colonel Theodore Roosevelt, who governed from 1929 to 1932, and Rexford Guy Tugwell, who governed from 1941 to 1946. After Guy Tugwell resigned, President Truman appointed the first Puerto Rican governor, Jesús T. Piñero. He was a close friend of Muñoz. Piñero served until 1948, when Muñoz became the first elected governor.

p. 78, *Dialogue in Pinto's account*: Gustavo Agrait, "Relatos favoritos," Luis Muñoz Marín Foundation Archives, booklet.

p. 78, *"I seal my promise"*: The author grew up listening to Puerto Ricans making promises in this manner.

PUERTO RICO, COMMONWEALTH OF THE UNITED STATES (1945–1964)

p. 79, *"There is . . . a man in tatters"*: Luis Muñoz Marín, "Rodinesca," in "Cantos de la humanidad forcejando," *Cuasimodo* 4 (June–July 1920).

p. 79, *Populares* is the name given to the members of the Popular Democratic Party.

p. 79, *Commonwealth—Dorfman account*: Teodoro Moscoso and Jorge Font Saldaña, "Cómo, cuando y por qué Muñoz Marín renunció a la prédica de la independencia," *El Nuevo Día* (Sunday, April 25, 1982).

p. 81, *The Puerto Rican Independence Party* was founded October 20, 1946. In 1948, it got 66,141 votes, or 10.4 percent of the 638,687 votes cast. The party has never won an election.

p. 81, *Commonwealth agreement (Public Law 600)*: As a Commonwealth, Puerto Rico continues its close ties with the United States, but it has its own Constitution. Puerto Ricans continue to be United States citizens, and do not pay federal taxes. If a draft is called, they have to serve in the military. But they cannot vote for the president of the United States. They receive benefits such as Social Security, but their only representation continues to be the resident commissioner, who cannot vote in Congress.

p. 81, *1951 referendum*: Of the 777,675 registered voters, 65.08 percent voted; and of those, 76.5 percent approved the agreement.

p. 83, *"Muñoz, where do you go from here?"*: Peggy Mann, *Luis Muñoz Marín: The Man Who Remade Puerto Rico* (New York: Coward, McCann & Geoghegan, 1976), 103.

p. 83, Jíbaro *culture*: Muñoz called his efforts to preserve the Puerto Rican culture Operation Serenity, perhaps because he thought it would give "serenity" to those who worried about losing their cultural roots.

p. 83, *"The battle for a good life"*: Earl Parker Hanson, *Transformation: The Story of Modern Puerto Rico* (New York: Simon & Schuster, 1955), 236.

p. 83, *Migration*: During the 1940s, the average net migration from Puerto Rico to the United States was 14,501. In the 1950s, however, it averaged 42,083, and it skyrocketed to 74,603 in 1953, after Puerto Rico became a Commonwealth.

p. 83, *"We should not agree with this continuing situation"*: Arturo Morales Carrión, *Puerto Rico: A Political and Cultural History*. (New York: W. W. Norton & Company, 1983), 288.

p. 83, *"People living in homes"*: Luis Muñoz Marín, "Al izar la bandera," San Juan (July 25, 1952), Commonwealth speech.

p. 84, *"Death to nobody!"*: Elfren Bernier, *Luis Muñoz Marín: Líder y Maestro* (Puerto Rico: Ramallo Brothers Printing, 1988), 345.

THE TWENTY-TWOS (1964–1980)

p. 85, *"Yesterday, I sang of strong things"*: Luis Muñoz Marín, "Moods," in *The Golden Magazine* (August 1926); *La juventud*, VIII.

p. 85, *Some of the Twenty-twos* were the sons and daughters of the Popular Democratic Party leaders. Others worked for Muñoz and the government. The Twenty-twos never elected a leader but worked as a group.

p. 86, *"My father didn't oppose my joining the Twenty-twos"*: María Soledad Calero, *Melo Muñoz: ¿Una nueva esperanza?* (Puerto Rico: NMC Editores, 1991), 46–47.

p. 86, *"No! Four more years!"*: Philip Sterling and María Brau, *The Quiet Rebels* (Garden City, N.Y.: Doubleday, 1968), 115.

p. 86, *"Forever keep your will"*: Luis Muñoz Marín, Barranquitas, August 1964, speech.

p. 86, *Roberto Sánchez Vilella*: After the election, Roberto Sánchez Vilella tried to build up power for himself by supporting the ideas of the young Populares. That created tension between the young and old leadership and weakened the Popular Democratic Party. Muñoz was still in the Senate and that secured the Commonwealth victory in the 1967 referendum. But the Republicans won the 1968 election.

p. 86, *"Muñoz was a joy!"*: Author's interview with Sergeant Julio Quirós, Río Piedras, July 28, 1992.

p. 88, *Dialogue with little girl*: Elfren Bernier, *Luis Muñoz Marín: Líder y maestro* (Puerto Rico: Ramallo Brothers, 1988), 314.

p. 89, *"So that you can go"*: Author's interview with Sergeant Julio Quirós, Río Piedras, July 28, 1992.

p. 89, *"Please, let's bury Muñoz"*: Author's interview with Sergeant Julio Quirós, Río Piedras, July 28, 1992.

p. 90, *"Muñoz gave up"*: Pedro A. Galarza: "Ante la tumba de Don Luis Muñoz Marín," Barranquitas, February 18, 1988, speech.

AFTERWORD

p. 91, *"Gone to feed the roots"*: Luis Muñoz Marín, "A Death," in "Queries," Poetry (between October 1924 and March 1925): 136–37; *La juventud*, 177.

p. 91, *The annual per capita income* in Puerto Rico averaged $5,825 in 1993. It was half that of the poorest state (Mississippi, $11,724) and a quarter of that of the richest state (Connecticut, $25,001).

p. 91, In 1993, the *unemployment rate* in Puerto Rico averaged 17.3 percent. *Crime* was also high: 958 murders.

p. 91, *Literacy rate*: In 1901, it was 23 percent. In 1940, it was 70 percent, and 88 percent in 1993.

p. 93, *Congress and Puerto Rico*: Some representatives from the states with the smallest populations don't like the idea of Puerto Rico becoming a state because the 3.7 million residents would entitle the island to at least six members in the House. That would be more than some of these states could have. Other Congress members are opposed to having a Spanish-speaking state in the Union. And others say that Puerto Rico would be a "welfare state." Because income levels are less than half those on the mainland, many Puerto Ricans would not have to pay federal taxes and would be eligible for more benefits than they receive now. Whenever statehood is mentioned, the American industries also put pressure on Congress and threaten to pull out of the island. U.S. companies with operations in Puerto Rico do not have to pay federal taxes on profits made on the island. The Commonwealth government also gives them a big break by exempting 90 percent of the island-earned profits from taxes.

p. 93, *"The great task"*: Luis Muñoz Marín, in *Poet in the Fortress* by Thomas Aitken (New York: New American Library, 1964), 224.

p. 93, *Dialogue during the 1939 rally*: Elfren Bernier, *Luis Muñoz Marín: Líder y Maestro* (Puerto Rico: Ramallo Brothers, 1988), 230.

Index

emigration to U.S., 83, 113

English, 4, 80; Muñoz Marín's ability with, 9, 12, 53; teaching in, 12, 17 (illus.), 61–62; use required, 12, 61, 62 (illus.), 80

Europe, Muñoz Marín's travels in, 86–87, 87 (illus.)

El Fanguito ghetto, 50 (illus.), 53–54, 76

Ferré, Luis, 78, 84, 111

Foraker Act, 5, 103

Free Associate State, 45–46, 80; see also Commonwealth of the United States

Galarza, Pedro, 74–75, 89–90

Georgetti, Eduardo, 21, 22–23, 27 (illus.)

governors of Puerto Rico, 85–86, 98; appointed, 5, 54, 103, 111; elected, 78

Greenwich Village, 32–35

Henna, Dr. Julio, 36, 38

hurricanes, 9, 12, 49, 53

Iglesias, Santiago, 5, 38–41, 40 (illus.), 52, 58, 84; helps *jíbaros*, 36, 50; joins Republicans, 43, 50–51, 107; Muñoz Marín breaks with, 43

illiteracy, 4, 45, 58–59, 61–62, 79; as voting disqualification, 20, 64, 103

independence, 4, 6, 51, 60, 61; barriers to, 45, 79, 80; Muñoz Marín gives up on, 80, 88; Muñoz Marín opposes, 55–56; Muñoz Marín supports, 45–46, 48, 49; see also autonomy

Independence bill, Muñoz Marín opposes, 55–56

industry, Puerto Rican, 4, 49, 76, 83, 88

jíbaros [*jíbaras*], 5, 12, 25, 39 (illus.), 64 (illus.), 82 (illus.); and land ownership, 60, 68, 73, 75 (illus.), 76; liberation of, 60, 89–90; Muñoz Marín's political alliance with, 58–59, 63, 67 (illus.), 67–68; Muñoz Marín's sympathy with, 14, 29, 41, 57, 62, 68, 69, 71–72, 81–83, 90, 94; poverty of, 49–50, 53,

54; schools for, 73–76; urbanization of, 53–54, 83, 88; and voting, 20, 35, 37, 58

job creation, 54, 73, 76, 91, 111

Johnson, Lyndon B., 84 (illus.)

Jones, William, 20

Jones Bill, 20, 21, 37

Juan Bobo, 24 (illus.), 25

Kennedy, John Fitzgerald, 83, 84 (illus.)

labor movement, 5

landowners, 12, 38, 47, 54, 68; obstruct voting process, 37, 38, 69–70

land ownership, 60, 68, 73, 75 (illus.), 78

law school (Georgetown), 19, 22, 26

Lee (de Muñoz), Muna, 32–33, 34 (illus.), 43, 44 (illus.), 46; marries Muñoz Marín, 33; quoted, 33, 45; separation and divorce, 45, 63, 110; supports family, 35, 47; works for women's suffrage, 46

Lenin, 33

Liberal Party: Muñoz Marín joins, 51, 52 (illus.); is expelled, 56

literacy, 12, 65, 74, 91, 114

"The Man with the Hoe," 29, 105; Muñoz Marín translates, 36

Marín de Muñoz, Doña Amalia, 2 (illus.), 4, 27 (illus.), 30 (illus.), 41, 43

Markham, Edwin, 29, 35–36, 105

Marx, Karl, 33

Mendoza, Doña Inés, 61–64, 64 (illus.), 77 (illus.), 86, 87, 88; advocate of women's rights, 64; lives with Muñoz Marín, 63, 110; marries, 63

money problems of Muñoz Marín family, 35, 44, 46–47, 63

Muñoz Lee, Luis, 43–44, 44 (illus.), 63

Muñoz Lee, Munita, 36, 43, 44 (illus.)

Muñoz Marín, José Luis Alberto, 40 (illus.), 69 (illus.), 70 (illus.); assassination attempt, 81; born, 1, 2 (illus.); childhood, 4, 6, 8 (illus.), 9–10, 13 (illus.); chronology of his life,

95–96; falls out of favor, 29–31, 43, 56, 57; final years, 88–89; becomes full-time writer, 28, 32, 35; funeral of, 89, 90 (illus.); generosity to political opponents, 7, 84; gives up poetry for politics, 41–42, 51, 63, 90; as governor of Puerto Rico, 78, 85–86, 98; receives Medal of Freedom, 83, 84 (illus.); fondness for parties, 19, 26, 28; as poet and writer, 10, 19, 26–31, 30 (illus.), 32, 35, 47; political principles of, 49, 51, 55, 56, 83–84, 86, 93–94; as politician, 29, 51–52, 63, 92 (illus.); in Puerto Rican senate, 52, 71; relations to his father, 23, 26–28, 27 (illus.), 31, 38, 41, 52 (illus.), 58; travels across U.S., 35, 48, 108

Muñoz Mendoza, Victoria, 73, 77 (illus.), 89; joins Twenty-twos, 86

Muñoz Mendoza, Viviana, 63, 77 (illus.), 86

Muñoz Rivera, Luis, 1–2, 2 (illus.), 10, 22 (illus.), 52 (illus.); elected to house of delegates, 10; funeral, 23–25, 23 (illus.); poetic ambitions of, 10, 19; as prime minister, 2; resident commissioner in the U.S., 16; sickness and death, 21–22; works for Puerto Rican independence, 1, 4, 103; writings of, 10, 45, 107

names, Puerto Rican form of, 17 (illus.), 18, 97

The Nation, 47

Nationalist Party, 55; attacks Muñoz Marín, 81; supports independence, 51

New Deal, 54

New York, 33, 35; emigration to, 83; Muñoz Marín's moves to, 9, 16, 26, 32, 46; travel to and from, 10

Operation Bootstrap, 73, 74 (illus.), 111

Operation Serenity, 113

overpopulation, 46, 76, 80, 93, 98

poetic circles: in New York, 33, 105; in Puerto Rico, 28–29

poetry: of Muna Lee, 33, 45; of Muñoz Marín, 1, 7, 11, 16, 19, 21, 25, 26, 32, 33, 37, 41, 43, 49, 57, 61, 66, 73, 79, 85, 91, 103; Muñoz Marín gives up for politics, 41–42, 51, 63, 90; of Muñoz Rivera, 10, 19

Political Campaigns, 45

Popular Democratic Party, 57–58, 76, 79, 109; first campaign, 60, 66–68; flag, 58, 59 (illus.); newspaper of, 65; victory of, 71–72

population growth, 49, 76, 80, 93; statistics, 98; *see also* overpopulation

poverty: in Puerto Rico, 4, 11–12, 47–48, 51, 53–54, 55, 57, 58, 79, 81, 93, 114; in U.S., 91, 93, 108

Presidential Medal of Freedom, 83, 84 (illus.)

public housing, 76–77

Puerto Rican Independence Party, 81

Puerto Rico: economic status, 80, 88, 91; history, 1, 95–96; Muñoz Marín on, 11, 47; Muñoz Marín returns to, 11, 36, 45, 48; outline of government, 99–101; strategic value of, 4; as U.S. colony, 1, 5, 10, 80

Quirós, Sergeant Julio, 86, 87 (illus.), 114

Republicans (Puerto Rican), 7–9, 50–51, 87, 91; hostility to Muñoz Marín and family, 7–9, 46; indifference to *jíbaros*, 37–38; join other parties, 10, 51

Revista de Indias, 32, 35

Riggs, Francis, assassination of, 54–55, 108; Muñoz Marín refuses to condemn, 55

"Rivera, Joe," 16–18, 17 (illus.)

Roosevelt, Eleanor, 53–54, 55 (illus.); meets Muñoz Marín, 53

Roosevelt, Franklin Delano, 53, 54

ruling class, 4; *see also* landowners

rural areas, 4, 88